I0213684

Demonology

POWERS
OF DARKNESS

*– the second of two studies dealing with
the spiritual world of* Angels *and* Demons.

by
KEN CHANT

DEMONOLOGY

POWERS OF DARKNESS

By Dr. Ken Chant

Copyright © 2012 *Ken Chant*
ISBN 978-1-61529-038-3
2012 Edition

Vision Publishing
1672 Main St. E 109
Ramona, CA 92065
1-800-9-VISION
www.booksbyvision.com

All rights reserved worldwide

No part of the book may be reproduced in any manner whatsoever without written permission of the author except in brief quotations embodied in critical articles of reviews.

A NOTE ON GENDER

It is unfortunate that the English language does not contain an adequate generic pronoun (especially in the singular number) that includes without bias both male and female. So *"he, him, his, man, mankind,"* with their plurals, must do the work for both sexes. Accordingly, wherever it is appropriate to do so in the following pages, please include the feminine gender in the masculine, and vice versa.

FOOTNOTES

A work once fully referenced will thereafter be noted either by "ibid" or "op. cit."

Contents

ABBREVIATIONS

Abbreviations commonly used for the books of the Bible are

Genesis	Ge	Habakkuk	Hb
Exodus	Ex	Zephaniah	Zp
Leviticus	Le	Haggai	Hg
Numbers	Nu	Zechariah	Zc
Deuteronomy	De	Malachi	Mal
Joshua	Js		
Judges	Jg		
Ruth	Ru	Matthew	Mt
1 Samuel	1 Sa	Mark	Mk
2 Samuel	2 Sa	Luke	Lu
1 Kings	1 Kg	John	Jn
2 Kings	2 Kg	Acts	Ac
1 Chronicles	1 Ch	Romans	Ro
2 Chronicles	2 Ch	1 Corinthians	1 Co
Ezra	Ezr	2 Corinthians	2 Co
Nehemiah	Ne	Galatians	Ga
Esther	Es	Ephesians	Ep
Job	Jb	Philippians	Ph
Psalm	Ps	Colossians	Cl
Proverbs	Pr	1 Thessalonians	1 Th
Ecclesiastes	Ec	2 Thessalonians	2 Th
Song of Songs	Ca *	1 Timothy	1 Ti
Isaiah	Is	2 Timothy	2 Ti
Jeremiah	Je	Titus	Tit
Lamentations	La	Philemon	Phm
Ezekiel	Ez	Hebrews	He
Daniel	Da	James	Ja
Hosea	Ho	1 Peter	1 Pe
Joel	Jl	2 Peter	2 Pe
Amos	Am	1 John	1 Jn
Obadiah	Ob	2 John	2 Jn
Jonah	Jo	3 John	3 Jn
Micah	Mi	Jude	Ju
Nahum	Na	Revelation	Re

Ca is an abbreviation of *Canticles*, a derivative of the Latin name of the *Song of Solomon*, which is sometimes also called the *Song of Songs*.

A WORLD OF WONDER

This is the second part of a fascinating adventure – a quest to penetrate the veil, to step into another dimension, to learn what is happening in the world of spirits.

Our quest is in two sections, the first dealing with the kingdom of light, and the second (this book) with the kingdom of darkness. You will find familiar things here; you may also find things that startle and amaze you. Unless you are already full of knowledge, I am sure the following pages will enrich your understanding of the place occupied by angels and demons in God's world. Even well-informed students may find themselves encountering here some new ideas, some new ways of looking at the realm of both good and evil spirits.

You will find no stories about angels or demons, except those that come out of the Bible. I have refrained from building doctrine either on my own experiences or those of others. The books I have read about angels and demons abound in such stories, but I find many of them unconvincing.

The devil and demons entice some writers to present as normal and necessary quite sensational behaviour and quite speculative notions. I am certain many of those conjectures are spurious, and much of the erratic behaviour reported by some authors is merely psychic. I have grave doubts even about some of the things I have observed in my own ministry of exorcism, let alone what I have seen in the ministry of others. So I resolved in these chapters to avoid personal testimony, and to stick to scripture.

I regret having had more discernible contact over the years with demons than with angels - yet I am confident the holy angels have been constantly and effectively active in my life, and I hope what I have written will show this, along with the honour and gratitude I feel toward them.

Writing these chapters has reinforced my belief that it is unwise to desire too much knowledge about either angels or demons. We should be content with what scripture tells us. To yearn for more is perilous, and may lead to deep deception. These chapters will serve you well if they do no more (nor any less) than sufficiently expose you to the world of angels to enhance your confidence in God, and to the world of demons to ensure your personal mastery over the devil and all his works.

For the rest, Henry David Thoreau's admonition may serve us all well -

Most people with whom I talk, men and women even of some originality and genius, have their scheme of the universe all cut and dried - very dry, I assure you, to hear, dry enough to burn, dry-rotted and powder-post, methinks - which they set up between you and them in the shortest intercourse; an ancient and tottering frame with all its boards blown off ... The wisest man preaches no doctrines; he has no scheme; he sees no rafter, not even a cobweb against the heavens. It is a clear sky ... (Yet your) scheme must be the framework of the universe; all other schemes will soon be ruins. The perfect God in his revelation of himself has never got to the length of one such proposition as you, his prophets, state. Have you learned the alphabet of heaven and can count three? Do you know the number of God's family? Can you put mysteries into words? Do you presume to fable the ineffable? Pray, what geographers are you that speak of heaven's topography? Whose friend are you that speak of God's personality? ... Tell me of the height of the mountains of the moon, or of the diameter of space, and I may believe you; but of the secret history of the Almighty, and I shall pronounce you mad. [1]

---

[1] A Week On The Concord And Merrimack Rivers; The Heritage Press, Norwalk CT, 1975; pg 55,56 ("Sunday"). This book appeared in 1849 and was the first of the only two of his books that were published in his lifetime (the other was Walden). Both books are extraordinary in their idyllic

Thoreau was a little cavalier in his dismissal of all dogma. It is foolish to reckon that no certainty about anything is possible. But he was true enough in rejecting those mad prophets who are certain about everything! Some honest ignorance will do us no harm. Moses had a good balance -

"The secret things belong to the Lord our God, but the things revealed belong to us and to our children for ever" (De 29:29)

Let God keep secret what he pleases; let us be content with what he reveals.

serenity, penetrating observation, and literary power, and since Thoreau's death they have had far-flung influence. His Week sold only about 300 of 1000 copies that were printed. It is said Thoreau observed ruefully that he had somewhat more than a thousand books in his library, of which seven hundred were written by himself!

PREFACE

IS THE DEVIL REAL?

Henry David Thoreau once said, "There is always room and occasion enough for a true book on any subject, as there is room for more light on the brightest day, and more rays will not interfere with the first."[2] You may require that apology to introduce this, yet another book on the powers of darkness. You may have read many such already. Can there be room or need for another? If this book is true, Thoreau would have us answer "Yes!" to both questions. There is certainly room, for truth is never redundant; and there is surely a need, for so much that has been written on the subject is nonsense. Here as nowhere else another warning by Thoreau is imperative -

"By dint of able writing and pen-craft, books are cunningly compiled, and have their run of success even among the learned, as if they were the result of a new man's thinking, and their birth were attended with some natural throes. But in a little while their covers fall off, for no binding will avail, and it appears that they are not Books or Bibles at all."[3]

Sadly, several foolish and fantastic books about demons have had "their run of success" in our time, and some who should have known better have run with them. But they are looking now a little tattered. The mask has slipped. Their cheating words are being exposed. It may now be time for some responsible writing. Will you find it here? Or will this be just another "cunning

---

[2]   Op. cit., pg 88.

[3]   Op. cit., pg 78.

compilation", flourishing for a time, only to perish by its own treacherous flaws? I hope not! I surely have not written a Bible, but perhaps you will reckon it at least a Book!

But that is not easy when you are dealing with the devil. What mystery! What murkiness! If we stumbled along indistinct paths as we searched for evidence of the angels, those inhabitants of light, how much more will we find ourselves groping for the truth about demons, those dwellers in darkness! Yet some rays do shine out of scripture. We are not left wholly in ignorance. Enough of the enemy is seen to enable us to identify and overthrow him.

At once that raises a question. Is he actually there? Perhaps after all, those flitting spectres are figments of our own imagination. Perhaps we are still children, fearfully tracing weird profiles among the shadows of the night, and seeing ghouls where there are none?

AN ANCIENT MYTH?

I would find it easy to reject the idea of a personal devil. How can an educated person be expected to believe in demons, witches, divinations, spells, incantations, and the like? The whole paraphernalia of demonology seems like a hangover from the dark ages, a primitive superstition, with no valid place (except as a curiosity of history) in the thinking of modern man.

Surely all this talk about a devil and demons should be banished from theology and relegated instead to mythology? Surely those people are right who argue that demonology darkens sound doctrine and affronts an intelligent approach to the claims of the gospel? How can this seeming accretion of fantasy and fable, of spooks and spirits, of ancient fears and foibles, have any relevance to the needs of the modern church?

Such a rejection of the devil and his minions, of course, is not entirely a recent development. Modern teachers, both inside and outside the church, who denounce demonology as an irrational relic of the past, are simply following the example of sundry ancient philosophers and savants. The Greeks and the Romans were not lacking in sceptics. Even the Jews had their Sadducees, who jeered at the idea of Satan, and were equally scornful of stories about angels.

I would like to join them. I would like to discard the notion of a kingdom of darkness. It is much more pleasing to think God reigns unchallenged, that there is only one supernatural kingdom, that the Father is gently leading man away from ignorant superstition into an informed and loving relationship with himself.

The image of angels and demons cluttering the skies and warring against each other is unsettling. It seems offensive to a clear apprehension of the kingdom of God. How much nicer to say that the notion of Satan was an invention of our forefathers, a superstitious attempt to blame something or someone for the bizarre and tragic events they witnessed each day. We may allow that they had need of such myths to explain the mysteries of life; but surely it is anachronistic to talk about demonic forces in our society?

How easy it would be to agree with such a dismissal of the devil! But in the end I cannot. Three things stand in the way: the Bible; Christ; and myself -

1. The Bible

Demonology is woven so deeply into scripture it cannot be unthreaded without destroying the very fabric of salvation. Beginning with the Serpent tempting Eve in the Garden, and concluding with the Dragon's torment in the Lake of Fire, demonology is part of the structure of every major doctrine in the Bible. If we cannot believe what scripture teaches about the kingdom of darkness, then we have no basis on which to believe what it teaches about the kingdom of God. Demonology may be difficult for the natural man to receive; but it is an integral part of the revelation God has given to his people. Destroy the doctrine of Satan and you destroy the whole Bible.

2. Christ

The witness of Jesus on this matter is serious and emphatic. He spoke freely and constantly about the devil and evil spirits. He openly cast out demons. He gave clear teaching about Satan and the dark hordes.

Some insist that Jesus simply accommodated himself to popular superstition. He himself (they say) knew better. He understood that Satan was fiction, but he yielded to the ignorant naivete of the people.

What an absurd argument! Jesus did not hesitate to rebuke false traditions or untruthful notions whenever he encountered them. He condemned the Sadducees for their naturalism, and for their rejection of the resurrection. He rebuked the Pharisees for their legalism and perversion of the Sabbath. Even when he knew his words would antagonise the crowds he did not restrain his rebuke of their errors.

When was Christ ever reluctant to proclaim the truth?

So it is inconceivable that he could have remained silent about the devil, let alone actively endorse a popular myth, if he had known that myth was nonsense.

Another alternative holds that while Jesus evidently did believe in the devil and demons, we know he was wrong. We know such things do not exist, and that Jesus merely reflected the ignorance of the society in which he lived. But we are educated and cultured. How can we be asked to believe such unscientific and superstitious legends?

If that is so, then doubt is cast upon the credibility of everything Jesus taught. His sayings about the devil were not incidental to his larger message; on the contrary, they were an integral part of his teaching, and they were among the basic motivations of his mission (Mt 12:22-30; 13:19,39; 25:41; Lu 10:17-20; Jn 8:44; 12:31; 14:30; 16:11; etc). If he was in error on such a fundamental matter, he could be in error on any matter. His claim to represent the truth would be invalidated. Do you acknowledge that Christ is the Son of God? Then his teaching on demonology must be true.

3. Myself

But perhaps more deeply (and, speaking as a man, more personally) I am ultimately driven by one compelling reason to accept the reality of evil spirits. What is that reason? Simply this: the alternative is too horrible!

If Satan does not exist, then evil must have its origin solely in the human heart. Human depravity is left with no source save man himself. But that is too awful to contemplate. That would make evil a mystery defying all explanation, a horror lacking any mitigation. As Dostoevski wrote in The Brothers Karamazov, "If the devil doesn't exist, but man has created him, he has created him in his own image and likeness" (5.4).

But the universal occurrence of sin, the insane mindlessness of vice, the deep cunning of human wickedness, the unrestrained violence of human cruelty - these things are all too monstrous to admit the claim that they arise in man unaided. If this were so, then we are depraved beyond all rescue, and the human race deserves nothing but bloody immolation.

The only message that shines with any hope for man is the biblical one, which ultimately ascribes all evil to the Prince of Darkness, who is called Satan. His overthrow by Christ has created a way for men and women to emerge from corruption, and to be renewed as perfect sons of God, the fit inheritors of Paradise.[4]

---

[4] Some years after writing the above paragraphs I came across the following from Martin Luther: "The wickedness of the devil is so great than no man can grasp it, nor is it possible for any human being to be so wicked in his own nature. For although a man is very wicked and intensely angry and does his very worst, he thoroughly wreaks his vengeance, pours out the vials of his wrath and rage, and then stops. But to one so wicked as to find one's pleasure and delight only in the

Continued from previous page...

misfortune of other people, in their lingering hunger, thirst, misery, and want, in the perpetration of nothing but bloodshed and treason, especially

in the lives of those who neither have done nor could do one any harm, this is the hellish and insatiable rage and fury of the wretched devil, of which human nature is incapable." (What Luther Says, Vol One, compiled by E. M. Plass; Concordia Publishing House, St Louis MO; 1959; selection #1156.

At first sight it might seem that Luther is too genial toward the history of man's cruelty to man. But not really. There has never been a tyrant so brutalised, so insatiably cruel, that he lacked all boundaries around his ferocity. Even the worst of men have had some friends, or family, or supporters around them who were generally immune from the bully's caprice. Any ruler whose tyranny was totally unbridled, who violently sought to crush all who ventured near him, would be branded utterly insane even by his fellow despots. He would himself soon be destroyed. The very nature of human society, and of our need for each other, restrains even the most evil of men.

Not so the devil. His malicious hatred is boundless. No breath of pity, no whisper of mercy, enters his soul. He strikes with callous disregard at young and old, weak and strong, holy and unholy alike. Were he not subject to the laws and authority of the Lord God, he would ruthlessly butcher us all - and indeed, he still strives to do so (1 Pe 5:8). Give him any opportunity, and like an enraged lion, his fang and claw will devour the unwary!

CHAPTER ONE

OUR ADVERSARY

Go, and catch a falling star,
Get with child a mandrake root,
Tell me, where all past years are,
Or who cleft the Devil's foot."

In those opening lines from his cynical poem on the infidelity of a beautiful woman, John Donne refers to several mysteries that greatly exercised the medieval mind: the nature of meteors; the human qualities of the mythical mandrake; the philosophical argument about the nature of time; and who clove the devil's foot?

Based on an ancient legend that Satan assumes the shape of a he-goat whenever he attends a witches coven, people have for centuries pictured him as a goat standing upright with a pitchfork. But (the old people whispered) he could never discard his goat's hoof; so no matter what disguise he wore, you could always recognise him by that unnatural cleft. And of course there have been countless other myths attached to Satan over the years.

None of those concern us, for we are not interested in fable, but in fact. So we have no care to answer Donne's question about the cloven hoof, except to say that the devil is no goat!

Nonetheless, we might well echo John Milton's more chilling question: Whence and what art thou, execrable Shape? (Paradise Lost, 1.681). We cry with the poet, "Who is this dread foe?"

I. UNDER GOD'S CONTROL

I have read somewhere that Martin Luther said, "The devil is God's devil!" He meant that Satan is irrevocably subject to the will, authority, and power of the Lord God. How absurd to imagine that the powers of darkness pose any real threat to God's dominion! God made Satan. God rules him. God will punish him.

I remind you of this, lest, as we come to talk about Satan, and about his malignity and might, you should become fearful, and begin to magnify him as a rival of the Father. Always remember that the devil is not eternal; he is a created being. He has an absolutely contingent existence. He cannot survive independently of God. The word and will of God sustain Satan as they do every other living thing. People who forget this are prone to fall into the error known as "dualism" - either in doctrine or in practice.

Some of the world's great religions have been built on a "dualistic" principle. One of the first, and probably the most famous, was the religion of Zarathustra[5]

Zarathustra was an ancient Persian prophet. He lived about the 6th century B.C. -

> "At the age of thirty, or a little later, Zarathustra had a life-changing religious experience in which he met Ahura-Mazda ('The Wise Lord'). This experience plus other revelations led him to become the prophet of a new, purified religion. Tradition says this new prophet was successful in converting King Vishtaspa, the ruler of East Iran, and found a powerful protector of the faith in Vishtaspa's son, Darius the Great. Zarathustra died at age seventy-seven ... He bitterly attacked the cult of the gods of popular religion, and promoted the worship of the one Spirit, Ahura-Mazda (later called Ormazd)."[6]

[5] Often known as Zoroaster, a Greek corruption of his name.

[6] Article Zoroastrianism, "Dictionary of the Christian Church", ed. J. D. Douglas, The Paternoster Press, Exeter, Devon, U.K.; 1974.

He taught that Ormazd was engaged in relentless
and perpetual combat with an equally powerful foe,
Ahriman, the chief agent of evil. Ormazd was the
author of truth, righteousness, order; while Ahriman
created deceit, unrighteousness, and disorder.
Zarathustra urged all good men to "join the battle
against Ahriman ... in preparation for the final
judgment involving the resurrection of the dead and
the confinement of the wicked to the regions of
torment. Each individual was to be judged
according to his deeds."[7]

Zarathustrian dualism was the dominant religion of Persia for more
than a thousand years, and it inspired a host of imitators, including
some early Christian sects who exalted the devil to a position of
equality with God. Some even ventured far enough to worship
Satan in place of God - which may be the significance of the
reference to a "synagogue of Satan" in Re 2:9.

You can still find elements of this belief scattered through the
church. There are many people who either believe that the devil is
almighty or at least act as though he is. They think of him as a
powerful god striving against the Lord, and imagine that he is
barely hindered even by all the power of heaven.

But the devil is no rival of God. There is no contest. Whatever
power Satan has is solely by permission of God.

There is a profound mystery here, and we shall be looking at it
later in more detail; but you must understand right from the
beginning that there is nothing dualistic about the Christian faith.
Scripture does not in any sense show Satan as an eternal, uncreated
being, independent of God and nearly equal to him in power. Far,
far from it. The biblical picture is not a binary one of two powerful

---

[7]   Ibid.F

gods striving for mastery. Always the devil is utterly subservient to the will and power of the Lord God. The Creator rules alone, serene, and entirely unthreatened.

There is another aspect of dualism that is still at work in the church. Dualism tends to see the material world as either created by the devil or at least ruled by him; consequently, everything physical is reckoned essentially evil. Dualism claims that goodness exists only in the spiritual world created by God, and that the kingdom of darkness dominates the visible universe - good and evil are thought of as having separate creators.

A corollary of those ideas is a rejection of the world, the flesh, or anything physical. Anything material is seen as corrupt and antagonistic to the spirit. Hence there is a strong tendency to asceticism, to reckon that God cannot be found in, and has no dealings with, the physical world. Echoes of these ideas are still evident in much Christian thinking, as I have shown in greater detail in another series in this course, Christian Life.

II. WAR IN HEAVEN

I have said that there is no contest between God and Satan (in the sense that the supremacy of God is beyond threat); nonetheless, there is a cosmic battle taking place between the kingdom of darkness and the kingdom of God: "Now war arose in heaven. Michael and his angels fighting against the dragon; and the dragon and his angels fought" (Re 12:7). The dimensions of this conflict lie beyond our capacity to measure. We are largely unaware of its existence. The battle wages beyond the realm of ordinary human perception and we would hardly be conscious of it at all if we did not have the revelation of scripture.

We encounter here the same kind of mystery that faced us when we tried to draw the veil aside on the realm of the angels. We catch a fleeting glimpse of a universe normally beyond human ken, a vast dimension in the creation of God, inhabited by spirit beings; a world filled with dynamic surging activity; a world apart from our own, and yet our world has become that other world's battlefield. Angels and demons alike are involved in the affairs of men. Our destiny and theirs are inextricably locked together.

How great is this conflict? How intense are its battles? What is the cost to heaven of victory? Ronald Wallace gives a concise yet graphic description of what is taking place in the spiritual dimension -

> "(Genesis teaches) that what has gone wrong with human life cannot be explained except on the presupposition of the invasion and infection of human life by some malignant power, whose hatred of God goes beyond anything of which man is capable on his own initiative (cp. Mt 13:28). At the climax of the Bible story we see Christ struggling, not simply to reform and repair the evil wills of men and call them back to God, but against some force of titanic proportions whose challenge to what is good demands an agonising and total response from God himself (1 Jn 3:8). Jesus' life is a struggle against one who is mighty (Mk 3:27); the hour of his agony is the climax of this struggle (Lu 22:53). Yet there is no question about his triumph (Lu 10:18). The devil must therefore be regarded as an alien personal force in the universe, which seeks to annihilate what God has created, to bring chaos where there is order, darkness where there is light; which defies God with superb hatred and pride; which manifests itself in human sin, especially in the opposition which Jesus met and overcame in the cross."[8]

[8]   Ibid. pg. 295.

I am gripped by one statement in the above paragraph: "We see Christ struggling ... against some force of titanic proportions whose challenge to what is good demands an agonising and total response from God himself." The reality of the war in heaven is exposed by the sweat, blood, and torture of Jesus. The awful death of the Son of God is the measure of the cost of victory to heaven.

How can this be? If Satan is subject to God's rule, if the kingdom of darkness is infinitely inferior to the kingdom of heaven, why is the war so terrible, the battle so fearful, the cost of victory so dreadful? Why does God not simply speak one word and obliterate the entire community of wickedness?

A. SUSTAINED DIGNITY

The question of why God allows Satan to go on existing, to remain free from imprisonment, and to have power, remains unanswered in the Bible - at least, in a formal sense. The Bible simply assumes everywhere that Satan does exist, and that he does have freedom and power to pursue his evil ends, although he remains ultimately under Divine restraint. Hence many aspects of the devil's relationship with God are unknown: we do not know his origin, nor what is his real identity, nor precisely when or how he fell from the favour of God, nor how he has built and maintained his kingdom. The Bible just accepts that these things are so. It is futile to seek finality on why God allows the kingdom of darkness to continue and flourish.

But I can make some suggestions –

1. Part of the reason undoubtedly lies in the freedom God has given his creatures, which includes the freedom to rebel and to remain in a state of rebellion until the appointed time of judgment. Freedom to disobey God would have no meaning if it did not include freedom to continue in disobedience. If a single act of disobedience resulted in immediate annihilation then real moral choice would be prevented, for the choice would then become a decision to die, not a decision to rebel. True moral choice can exist

only when opportunity is given for the results of that choice to be consciously experienced.

Furthermore, if God destroyed each sinner the moment he sinned, then divine justice would seem capricious and selfish. It would never be known that the motive behind the Father's hatred of sin is not the preservation of his own supremacy, but the love he has for his creatures. He understands the intrinsic value of righteousness, and the dark horror of unrighteousness. But angels and men can perceive this only as they see righteousness and unrighteousness actually worked out in experience. By observing the outcome of obedience and of rebellion in the experience of those who have chosen one or the other, the whole creation is brought to understand this rule: God must, for the true happiness of heaven and earth, ultimately annihilate all that is wicked, and preserve alone that which is good.

So by allowing godliness and ungodliness to continue side by side, and the fruits of both to accumulate together, the Father has made it possible for his servants to understand the true nature of righteousness and to pursue it, not merely to escape death, nor just out of fear, but for its own sake, and with love.

Conversely, the wicked, observing the sickening harvest of their rebellion, will have no answer to give on the day of judgment, but will have to acknowledge the justice of the divine sentence against them.

Another aspect of this idea is that evil is not always immediately recognised as such. Even Satan can sometimes appear as an "angel of light", and iniquity frequently remains unrecognised until it has brought forth its full harvest. So again the principle holds: if evil or its agents were always destroyed at the moment of their birth, the judgments of God would appear arbitrary and unreasonable. Many would conclude that God is vindictive and malicious, making no distinction between good and evil.

So it seems inevitable that if God is going to give to his creatures freedom to rebel, he must allow them room to continue in rebellion

- if they choose to do so. But if judgment on sin can properly be delayed for a moment, then it can be delayed for a millennium, while the larger purposes of God are fulfilled.

It is obvious enough that judgment must wait for its appointed time; for if God were obliged to destroy immediately everything that was evil, or that caused evil, his purpose for his creation would be deeply frustrated. Which leads me to a second suggestion -

2.   The formation of the kingdom of darkness, and the presence of evil in the world, cannot prevent the realisation of the purpose of God -

He does whatever he pleases in heaven and on earth ... Surely the wrath of men shall praise thee ... For this purpose I have let you live, to show you my power, so that my name may be declared throughout all the earth (Ps 135:6; 76:10; Ex 9:16-17).

The Lord's great plan for his creation will be totally completed in the time he has appointed.

Picture the purpose of God as a great ocean liner following its charted course across the ocean. The ship will certainly reach port. But whether the voyage is pleasant or unpleasant will depend on the behaviour of its passengers. The captain cannot compel them to be nice to each other. Yet despite personal conflicts, or even if he has to imprison some passengers, the captain will not slow the ship nor alter his course. When the harbor is reached, the troublemakers will face trial and imprisonment, but the other passengers will gain the happiness of their journey's end.

So is the purpose of God. Who can thwart it? When he made the heavens and the earth and all that is in them, the Father had already fixed his plan. At that time he determined the ultimate destiny of his creation, and he set the agenda for each stage in his grand design. Nothing man or devil can do can turn aside the outworking of the divine strategy.

3.   When he devised the rules that control heaven and earth, the Lord established various causes, and he determined the

effects those causes would produce. About these laws of cause and effect, notice that

- ◆ their outworking cannot retard the greater and all-encompassing purpose that God has set in motion for the entire universe.

- ◆ God does not interfere with the normal effects of the causes he has created; to do so would be capricious, and it would disturb the stability and order of the universe. Even when a miracle takes place (that is, when God invades the natural order and performs a supernatural act) it could be argued that he is still doing no more than responding to a new cause (faith) by the proper effect (a miracle). But in any case, every day millions of God's creatures make all kinds of decisions, begin all kinds of actions, and reap the inevitable effects, without any direct involvement by God. The Lord turns aside the ordinary laws of cause and effect only in direct response to faith, or as an occasional necessity of his own will (cp. Ex 3:2; Nu 22:28; 17:8; 1 Sa 6:19; etc).

- ◆ because God has created freedom, he is obliged also to allow rebellion as a possible cause, and he cannot ordinarily deny its effects in slavery, sin, disease, misery, and the like. But the folly of fallen angels and men acting on this cause, and now suffering the inevitable effect, cannot prevent God from fulfilling his grand design to "bring many sons to glory!" (He 2:10).

God's proper refusal to interfere with his own laws of cause and effect, or to alter the freedom he has given his creatures, or to abrogate the destiny he has appointed for both angels and men, compels him to sustain all things as they are. Hence the devil continues his rampage among the nations and his war against the holy angels. Sin flourishes, and its resultant misery falls upon the whole family of man. Tragedy strikes impartially at both the righteous and the unrighteous (Lu 13:1-5). This state will continue until the appointed hour of judgment has come.

4. Within the same framework of stern adherence to his own laws, God permits Satan to retain a large measure of the dignity accorded him at the beginning, so that even an archangel must show him due respect (Jude 9). Hence Christ could not arbitrarily destroy Satan (as a capricious tyrant would do), but rather had to find a judicial means of nullifying his power and of achieving a sentence of judgment against him. That means was his own anguish at Calvary.

Thus the Lord God showed that nothing can provoke him to break the laws he himself has made. Others may violate the rules; but heaven steadfastly adheres to them. The powers of darkness may fall to obscenity and railing against even the highest dignity (2 Pe 2:9-11); but the Creator maintains respect for his creatures, even those who, as Satan himself, have most wickedly rebelled.

This astonishing Divine rectitude prevents God from ever acting maliciously, or with selfish vengefulness. Whatever God does must be an act of true justice, and of fulfilled righteousness, in harmony with his own holy law. The adherence of the Godhead to this rule by law is so absolute that the Father did not scruple to commit his Son to Calvary. Nor did Christ refuse to plunge into the blackness of death. Sin had to be conquered. The power of Satan had to be nullified. Death had to be destroyed. The kingdom of darkness had to be lawfully overthrown. Alone, Jesus trod the winepress of the justice of God; and on the cross he made an open show of the devil, triumphed over him, and led captivity captive (Is 63:1-3; Cl 2:15; Ep 4:8).

We might still wonder why God did not simply utter one word and obliterate in a moment all the hosts of wickedness. But the cross shows that there is a mystery in iniquity, a magnitude to the war in heaven, a depth to the justice of God, that human understanding cannot penetrate. We must be content to trust in the finality of the triumph Christ has gained over Satan. Scripture promises that all evil will one day be driven out of God's world, and that heaven's victory will be gained lawfully, not by an arbitrary use of superior power.

5. Within this righteous framework of adherence to his own laws, the Lord God permits Satan to build a kingdom and to maintain his authority over it. Jesus spoke of the devil's kingdom and showed that Satan ruled it with intelligence and order. His kingdom is not divided. His servants are obedient to his will. They wage war with him against the majesty of heaven. They maintain their proper ranks and divisions. See Matthew 12:25-27, where Jesus insists that no discord tears at Satan's kingdom; on the contrary it is united in its purpose and in its subservience to its master.

This unity of purpose and strength indicates the vast intelligence and awesome power of Satan. The Lord God himself has respect for the majesty of his creature, Satan, and he will not ally himself with the fault of the devil by doing violence to his own decrees. Having made the devil glorious in the beginning, though he is now in a fallen and rebellious state, the Lord adheres to the mandate he gave Satan, and he will not abrogate that mandate until the hour of judgment comes. But neither does the Lord allow the devil to exceed his mandate. Hence Satan is honoured yet condemned; free yet fettered; mighty yet weak - but this is a matter for later discussion.

B. DELAYED JUDGMENT

What I have written above may explain why God has allowed Satan and his minions (both demons and men) so much freedom of activity, but it does not explain why judgment has been so long delayed, why God has chosen to wait so long before pouring out his wrath upon iniquity and inaugurating his kingdom of righteousness. There are two reasons for this delay -

1. Iniquity Must Be Full

"The iniquity of the Amorites is not yet full," God told Abraham (Ge 15:16), and thus revealed a principle that governs the judgments of God: that is, judgment cannot fall until sin has so developed that all possibility of repentance is past. It is the law of "blasphemy against the Holy Spirit" -

> *"I tell you, every sin and every blasphemy will be forgiven men, but the blasphemy against the Spirit will not be forgiven. And whosoever speaks a word against the Son of man will be forgiven; but whoever speaks against the Holy Spirit will not be forgiven, either in this age or in the age to come" Mt 12:31-32).*

Every other sin can be forgiven because every other sin leaves room for repentance; but to blaspheme the Holy Spirit is to resist the only possible influence that can produce repentance; it is to take on the very nature of sin; the blasphemer becomes rooted forever in iniquity. Nations, men, and demons can so far advance into wickedness, into rejection of the will of God, that repentance becomes truly impossible. But until the wicked reach that place of total depravity, God withholds the final sentence of doom.

There are indications in scripture that this principle (of iniquity reaching full fruition before final sentence is passed) is applicable to Satan. The OT pictures the devil as a less malicious creature than he is in the NT. He is still the tempter, a liar from the beginning, and a murderer (Jn 8:44), and he still seeks to harm the children of God (Job ch. 1-3; 1 Ch 21:1); but he does not loom in the OT, as he does in the NT, as an insatiably wicked opponent of God and of the church. In fact the reticence of the OT about Satan is as remarkable as the frequency the comments and denunciations of the devil in the NT.

The noun "Satan" is used in Ps 109:6; Job 1:2.; Zc 3:1, in the sense of an opponent at law, a legal "adversary", whose function it is to demand the condemnation of an accused person. It is also used in 1

Ch 21:1 in the sense of an enemy stirring up trouble. In none of those places does it have the utterly sinister and evil sense that it has everywhere in the NT.

You will find further confirmation in the way the OT uses the same noun in other quite ordinary settings (Nu 22:22; 1 Sa 29:4; 2 Sa 19:22; 1 Kg 5:4; 11:14,23,25), whereas the NT uses "Satan" invariably as a proper name for the arch-enemy of God and man. In the OT, Satan is numbered among the "sons of God", and he appears to have lawful and proper access to heaven, even to the very throne of God. He seems to be a minister of God, having a specific duty "to go to and fro on the earth" (Jb 1:6-7) and to report on the conduct of such people as God may designate. He is indeed rebuked by the Lord for an excess of zeal, even malice, in the prosecution of his task (Zc 3:2); nonetheless he seems to have right of access to the throne and of prosecuting a complaint.

The little notice taken of Satan in the OT, in marked contrast with the NT, along with the milder character portrayed, may indicate that he was then less an enemy of the people of God than he later became. Perhaps his depravity was not complete in the beginning, but he gradually grew in viciousness and in the intensity of his hatred of God.

Even now this process may be continuing, for the scriptures imply that the hatefulness of the devil will not be fully developed until the end of the age is near -

> *Woe to you, O earth and sea, for the devil has come down to you in great wrath, because he knows that his time is short (Re 12:12).*

His time will be short, because with the full development of his iniquity the judgment of God must soon fall upon him. This growing wickedness of Satan, and of his demonic hordes, is the cause of the increasing tribulation that scripture says will trouble the earth in the latter days.

But the word is sure: though God may delay judgment "until the iniquity of the Amorites is full," when that fullness is reached, the wrath of God must fall. As it fell on the kingdom of the Amorites, so will it on the kingdom of darkness.[9]

2. The Family Of God Must Be Completed

I saw four angels standing at the four corners of the earth, holding back the four winds of the earth ... Then I saw another angel ascend from the rising of the sun .. . saying, `Do not harm the earth or the sea or the trees, till we have sealed the servants of our God upon their foreheads.' And I heard the number of the sealed, a hundred and forty-four thousand (Re 7:1-4).

The sixth chapter of Revelation ends with an anticipation of awful judgment about to fall upon the whole earth. But when it seems that doom is inevitable, and that sudden, unrestrained destruction will bring about the end of the age and the consummation of all things, a new and startling scene interrupts the vision. John sees an angel coming out of the east and bidding the angels of wrath to stay their hands until the purpose of God for his people is fully accomplished - and in particular, until the number of the redeemed is complete. Albert Barnes comments -

---

[9]   But compare the following different viewpoint: "A simpler explanation of the history of the doctrine of the personality and agency of Satan is that it has been the subject of development under the influence of progressive revelation. The complete revelation of such a being as the malignant author of evil was reserved for the time when, with the advent of Christ's kingdom, the minds of God's people were prepared, without risk of idolatry, or of the mischievous dualism of such a religion as that of Zoroaster, to recognise in the Serpent of Eden and in the Satan who appeared as the adversary of Job and Joshua, the great Adversary of God and man, whose power is to be feared, and his temptations resolutely resisted, but from whose dark dominion the Son of God had come to deliver mankind." Article, "*Satan*", "Dictionary of Christ and the Gospels", edited by James Hastings, Vol. 2; Baker Book House, Grand Rapids, Michigan; 1973 reprint; pg. 570.

"This furnished an opportunity of disclosing a glorious vision of those who will be saved ... The fact, as seen in the symbol, is that the end of the world does not come at the opening of the sixth seal, as it seemed as if it would, and as it was anticipated in the time of consternation. The number of the chosen was not complete, and the impending wrath was therefore suspended. God interposes in favour of his people, and discloses in vision a vast number from all lands who will yet be saved, and the winds and storms are held back as if by angels."[10]

Here then is a passage of scripture telling us that the major factor causing God to delay the act of judgment is the finalising of the number of his people. The servants of God must first be numbered and marked; the total family of God must be gathered together; the Lord must first secure all his designated children; then the wrath will come (cp also Ez. 9:4-6).

I take it that the 144,000 are synonymous with the "great multitude which no man could number, from every nation, from all tribes and peoples and tongues, standing before the throne and before the Lamb, clothed in white robes" (Re 7:9-12; and cp. 14:1-5). The servants of God are represented both figuratively and literally. Actually, they comprise an immense multitude, beyond calculation; yet their number is pre-determined by God. He has counted them all, from the first redeemed man, Adam, to the last still to be won for Christ. God knows all those who are his; he knows how many he has resolved shall be in his family, and of those whom he has named as his own, and who have also named him their God, the Father will lose none.

---

[10]   Notes on the New Testament; one volume reprint, 1966, by Kregel Publications, Grand Rapids, Michigan, USA; pg 1600.

When the Father's family has reached its appointed limits, then the end will come.

You may ask, "Is the limit determined by the will of man or of God?" I suppose that human and divine will are both involved in this matter. On the one hand, God has undoubtedly determined how many sons he will lead home to glory (He 2:10); on the other hand, each of us must resolve for ourselves whether or not we will be in that company (Re 22:17). But this is a great mystery.[11]

C. DIVINE PROVIDENCE

Let me say it again: no activity of Satan can hinder God's purpose. On the contrary, the devil is obliged to serve the purpose of God, sometimes consciously, sometimes without realising what he is doing. I will return to this theme later, when I deal with our redemption, but for now the following comment by J. Barton Payne is helpful -

> "Most instructive of all is the multiple motivation when Satan is involved as well as sinful men. David, for example, ordered the census because of his false trust in armies (2 Sa 24:3,4); Satan, at the same time, moved David to do this because of his own hatred for God's people, Israel (1 Ch 21:1); but Satan's maliciousness became God's tool for his righteously angry punishment of the wayward people of Israel (2 Sa 24:1). Furthermore, although the reason for God's anger is not explicitly stated, it presumably arose because of Israel's sinful desertion of Yahweh's anointed at the time of Absalom's rebellion against David, which God in turn had ordered so as to punish David for his sin with Bath-sheba (2 Sa 12:11), and which God then

---

[11]   See the lesson four of the Great Words series, "Predestination."

overthrew because of Absalom's pride and wickedness (17:14)! Again, in the case of the plundering of Job, the motivation of the Sabeans against Job was one of greed for the plunder (Job 1:15), but Satan used their greed to further his own ends of opposition to God and to his elect (vs. 9-11). Simultaneously, however, God had ordained this same distinctive act, though with his own righteous motive of proving Job. God thus made use of the sinful motivations of both of the other parties to accomplish his over-all goal. `Surely the wrath of men shall praise thee, and the remainder of wrath shalt thou restrain!'"[12]

Here is both the majesty and the mystery of the providence of God. He who is at war with heaven, is also heaven's slave. Satan can do nothing that does not ultimately bring the purpose of God closer to fulfilment. Yet he and his demon hordes appear to wreak awful havoc and harm among the people of God. He is a foe to be feared; yet he is also thoroughly defeated for even the weakest of God's children. There are aspects of this mystery that we may never penetrate. But the majesty of God we can readily comprehend. We can boldly affirm that Satan is God's servant more than he is God's enemy, and that the kingdom of darkness can never avoid nor thwart the sovereignty of God. Always God is working out his own will. Never doubt "that in everything God is working for good with those who love him, who are called according to his purpose" (Ro 8:28).

[12]   The Theology of the Older Testament; Zondervan Publishing House, Grand Rapids, Michigan, USA; 1975; pg. 199-200

D. THE WITNESS OF CHRIST

The most potent testimony on the existence of the Devil, and of the warfare being waged between heaven and hell, was given by Jesus himself. He openly spoke about the satanic kingdom and its relentless onslaughts against the kingdom of God. He knew that the cost of victory would be no less than the supreme sacrifice of his own life and his own descent into hades. He shrank from drinking that terrible cup, and from the awful anguish it would demand from him. But he remained obedient to his Father's will, he entered into the terrible struggle, and almost at once his face was stained with the blood of battle -

> `Father, if thou art willing, remove this cup from me; nevertheless, not my will, but thine, be done' ...*
> *And being in an agony he prayed more earnestly; and his sweat became like great drops of blood falling down upon the ground (Lu 22:42-44).*

In this dreadful conflict he had some support from the angels of heaven (vs. 43) - but essentially he had to fight alone. The dark mystery of iniquity, the terrible power of hell, the almost infinite cost of victory, are all exposed in Gethsemane and at Calvary. Were Satan not real, and his power not beyond human measure, righteousness could have triumphed at a price far less bitter.

Jesus identified his awesome foe: "the enemy ... is the devil" (Mt 13:39); he also called him Satan and Beelzebul, and spoke of his kingdom (12:25-27). He knew that Satan was toiling in a frenzy to destroy both him and the mission God had given him (4:1-11), and that this dread enemy would lose no opportunity to overthrow the Christ (Lu 4:13). He announced that he had come from heaven to earth especially to pursue the war against hell and to destroy the works of the devil; even the demons themselves were aware of this, and hated him for it (Mk 1:24-25,34; Mt 12:24-27; Lu 10:17-19; and cp. He 2:14; 1 Jn 3:8).

The battle was engaged, and won, at Calvary -

Christ disarmed the principalities and powers and made a public example of them, triumphing over them in the cross (Cl 2:15).

Yet the war has not ended. God permits the kingdom of darkness to continue its attack upon the saints; the devil perpetuates his hatred of all that is godly; and we are warned to

"...be sober, be watchful, (for) your adversary the devil prowls around like a roaring lion, seeking someone to devour" (1 Pe 5:8).

But if we resist him, standing firm in faith, then we are assured that he will flee from us, defeated (vs. 9; Ja 4:7).

CHAPTER TWO

THE ORIGIN AND FALL OF SATAN

"Talk of the devil, and you'll hear his bones rattle," says an old Danish proverb. But we intend to talk about him nonetheless, and he may rattle his bones as much as he pleases, for we fear him not. But neither do we despise him. There is not much sense in another old proverb (this time English), which says, "The devil is an ass!" Arrogant, he may be, and insane to rebel against God, but he remains shrewd, powerful, and able to crush the unwary.

We are fully safe only while we stand firm in the name of Jesus, trusting the promises of God, protected by the blood of the cross.

But in that immunity, let us go deeper into the kingdom of darkness, and answer the questions: Who is Satan? Where did he come from?

Throughout the infrequent references to the devil in the OT and the frequent references to him in the NT, there is a common theme: Satan is the tempter, the deceiver, the thief, the destroyer. But how did he come to this unrighteous character? Was he made this way from the beginning? Is his enmity against God an involuntary, original element in his nature, or did he come to the role of adversary by personal choice?

The lack of biblical data makes those questions, and others like them, difficult to answer. It may not even be wise to delve too deeply into satanic origins. Undue curiosity about the kingdom of darkness may turn the soul into a prey for demons.

However, certain things are generally believed by the Church, based either on direct statements in scripture, or on inference

- men and angels were both created to obtain a perfect vision of God, to come into loving fellowship with the Father, and to receive a glorious inheritance. But those things cannot be gained without a time of probation and testing.

- the angels were "created as pure spirits, endowed with supernatural life", but a certain number of them failed to pass their probationary test, hence God banished them from heaven.

- it is usually held that one chief angel, variously called the Devil, Satan, Lucifer, Beelzebub, seduced the rest who fell with him from grace and into the regions of darkness.

- the nature of the sin committed by the fallen angels is a matter of conjecture, except that it is usually thought to have been some form of self-assertion - perhaps of seeking equality with God; or of supplanting the position and prerogatives of Christ; or of obtaining the beatific vision by self-effort instead of Divine grace.

- the immediate cause of this rebellion may have been envy of the position and honour God was intending to give to the crowning achievement of his creation, that is, to man, made in the image of God. There was a mystery and glory attached to this Divine likeness in man that not even the highest angel could hope for. Perhaps Satan desired to eliminate from the very beginning this threat to his own pride. That was the opinion of the writer of the ancient Book of Wisdom: "God made man imperishable, he made him in the image of his own nature; it was the devil's envy that brought death into the world, as those who are his partners will discover" (2:23, Jerusalem Bible).

- the early church accepted the teaching of the OT on Satan, and also the Jewish development of that teaching; thus the demonology of the NT is much more complex than that of the OT, but it closely follows the teachings and traditions of contemporary Judaism.

In brief, the NT describes Satan as

♦ a malevolent personal being, full of cunning, immensely strong, who is the prince of evil spirits, or demons (Mk 3:22; Ep 2:2; Re 12:7-9; and cp. Mt 25:41);

♦ he is one of the angels who did not keep to his first proper place, but sought to usurp a position that did not belong to him (Ju 6; 2 Pe 2:4);

♦ he is the chief enemy of man, and our accuser before God (Re 12:10; plus the prologue of Job, and Zc 3:1-2);

♦ for a brief time (in contrast with eternity) he has great power in this world (Re 12:12); therefore scripture calls him "the god of this age" (2 Co 4:4; cp. Jn 14:30; 16:11).

♦ the kingdom of darkness is at war against both the angels and mankind; it wars against man by infliction of misery and by enticement to evil - but only rarely, if ever, is Satan permitted by God to tempt men and women directly; rather, he is obliged to work through such second causes as the human body and its appetites.

♦ the final overthrow of the kingdom of darkness is certain, and in the meantime God still reigns supreme, and Satan and his minions can do nothing unless God allows it.

Perhaps my cautious reluctance to express an opinion about the origin and identity of Satan surprises you. You may have accepted the popular notion that he was once a most glorious archangel, who became proud and was cast out of heaven. That may be correct. But scripture is largely silent on the matter. Even Martin Luther (who was not always so reticent) wrote warily on this subject -

"These are the assured facts: the angels fell, and the devil was turned into an angel of darkness from an angel of light ... Let it then suffice for us to know that there are good and evil angels, but that God created them all equally good. Thence it follows of necessity that the evil angels fell and did not stand firm in the truth. But how this happened is not known."[13]

Yet even in those circumspect remarks Luther goes beyond scripture, which nowhere tells us that Satan was once "an angel of light"! Well then, what does the Bible say?

I. THE SERPENT IN THE GARDEN

The first mention of Satan in scripture is usually reckoned to be the story of the Serpent tempting Adam and Eve - although in the story itself the Serpent is not identified as Satan. However, it must be a fair inference that Satan and the Serpent are identical, especially in the light of Re 12:9, where Satan is described as "the great dragon, that ancient serpent, who is called the Devil, and Satan, the deceiver of the whole world." The words of Ro 16:20 also seem to refer right back to God's curse upon the Serpent, that "the seed of the woman" would "bruise (his) head" (Ge 3:15).

How should this story be read? Literally or figuratively? Did a real snake speak to Adam and Eve? Are snakes today really under a continuing curse of God? Or is the presence of a serpent in the story only a literary device, a spiritual symbol?

A. THE STORY IS LITERAL

Those who claim that the story in Genesis 3 must be taken literally argue thus -

> "That a real serpent was present in the garden is shown ... by its comparison with the other animals

---

[13]   Op. Cit. selection # 1149.

(3:1), as well as by the direct reference to the snake in God's subsequent curse (vs.14). The snake's presence, moreover, is confirmed by the witness of the NT (2 Co 11:3). But behind the visible serpent there lay an equally real, spiritual personality ... The NT makes (a) specific identification of the snake with the person of Satan (Ro 16:20; Re 12:9). The underlying presence of Satan is further borne out by the nature of the curse. The serpent was indeed more seriously condemned than all the other animals (Ge 3:14; for they too were about to suffer under the curse upon nature, vs. 17; cp. Ro 8:22). This beast's motion upon its belly would henceforward signify the failure of its attempt to exalt itself against man, as well as its fate of being trampled and crushed (Ge 3:15). But its curse was to be a perpetual curse: `all the days of its life' (vs. 14). The rest of God's natural creatures will some day be freed from the curse (Ro 8:21), but even in the redeemed kingdom of the testament of peace, the serpent will still be `eating dust' (Is 65:25). The reason for this unique degradation of the serpent seems to lie in the correspondingly eternal punishment that remains in store for its master, Satan (Re 20:3,10)."[14]

In that view, while Satan is recognised as the evil genius who inspired and controlled the serpent, there is still a clear belief that the serpent was real, that he did speak to Eve, that he was cursed by God, and that this class of reptile still abides under God's judgment, and will continue under a sentence of degradation for ever.

---

[14]   Dr. J. Barton Payne, The Theology of the Older Testament, Zondervan Publishing House, Grand Rapids, Michigan, 1975 reprint, pg. 291/293.

Associated with those ideas you will often hear that before the pronouncement of the Divine curse, the Serpent was not only the most subtle of creatures, but also the most beautiful. Only after the curse were snakes changed into their present shape, presumed stupidity, and lowly method of locomotion.

However, the story itself offers no suggestion of those things.

Keil and Delitzsch present a modified version of a literal reading -

> "The `serpent' is said to have been the tempter. But to anyone who reads the narrative carefully in connection with the previous history of the creation, and bears in mind that man is there described as exalted above all the rest of the animal world ... (and that) no help meet for him was found among the beasts of the field, and also that this superiority was manifested in the gift of speech, which enabled him to give names to all the rest - a thing which they, as speechless, were unable to perform - it must be at once apparent that it was not from the serpent, as a sagacious and crafty animal that the temptation proceeded, but that the serpent was simply the tool of (Satan)".[15]

> In that view, the serpent, at the time of the temptation, bore much the same appearance as snakes do today, and the act of speaking was a diabolic miracle of the same class as the divine miracle that caused Balaam's ass to speak. Martin Luther held to this opinion -"We must ... let it stand that what the woman saw with her eyes was a real, natural serpent ... But the devil dwelt in it, because

[15] Commentary on the Old Testament, Vol. 1, The Pentateuch; William B. Eerdman's Publishing Co., Grand Rapids, Michigan, 1976 reprint, pg. 91/92.

Moses says that it talked with her (Ge 3:1- 6). For speaking is not an endowment of any animal, but only of man. Thus Moses makes it clear enough to our understanding that the devil in the serpent spoke through its tongue. And this should not surprise anybody, for the devil is a powerful spirit."[16]

However, despite his avowed intention of not going beyond scripture, Luther certainly does so in that place. For scripture nowhere says that the devil spoke through a lowly snake, but simply declares: Now the serpent was more subtle than any other wild creature that the Lord God had made. He said to the woman, `Did God say, You shall not eat of any tree of the garden?'... " According to Genesis, the serpent himself spoke to the woman

B. THE STORY IS SYMBOLIC

The literal view presents difficulties:

- ♦ if the serpent was a reptile similar to modern snakes, then it is incredible that it could talk, and even more incredible that Eve should accept its speech without the slightest sign of surprise.

- ♦ the biology of reptiles does not accord with the biblical description of the serpent being "more subtle than any other wild creature" (for snakes have a low intelligence), nor of them "eating dust" (for they are carnivorous), nor of them being deadly to man (for many of them are non-venomous, and some of them are singularly beautiful, deserving as much admiration as any other part of God's creation). Many other animals and insects wreak more havoc on human life than snakes have ever done.

---

[16]   Op. Cit. selection # 1153.

♦ if the serpent in Genesis 3 was radically superior to modern reptiles, to the extent of being able to talk, it is astonishing that no mention was made of this when Adam was naming all the creatures and seeking a companion.

♦ if the Devil took possession of a serpent, and spoke through him, then why should a curse be pronounced on the reptilian race, which after all were helpless tools of Satan? In any case, snakes do not appear to be faring any better or any worse than any other member of the animal species; there is no apparent sign that they are under a curse any greater than affects the whole creation because of sin.

For such reasons, other commentators prefer a more figurative reading of the story. Hence James Inglis writes -

> "There is another view which, while it supposes the devil to be the agent in effecting the temptation, regards what is said respecting the serpent to be figurative, just as the Apostle Paul says, 'The serpent beguiled Eve' (2 Co 11:3), when undoubtedly he means that the devil beguiled her. In this view the real facts of the case are represented under the veil of allegory. There was no serpent nor any appearance of one. The serpent is selected to represent the devil on account of its proverbial cunning; and that part of the curse which is generally supposed to have been denounced against the reptile itself was in fact meant for the devil ... "

Inglis does not agree with this extreme symbolism, so he continues-

> "What appeared to Eve seemed to be a serpent, and is described accordingly ... Whether there was a real serpent, or only the likeness of one, is not so easy to determine ... The apostle speaks of Satan as being transformed into an angel of light (2 Co 11:14), and he may have had the power of assuming the form of

a serpent ... The question is not determined by such expressions as `the serpent said', for as angels are called men, so may the tempter be called a serpent without his being a real serpent ... "[17]

Inglis goes on to argue that the passage does not talk about a creature that was no more than a common member of the general class of snakes, but rather a particular "serpent", solitary, unique -

"It is this serpent, not the serpent kind, but this serpent only that is cursed. When it is said, `I will put enmity between thy seed and her seed,' the reference is certainly to nothing so insignificant as the aversion of men to serpents. The natural inference is, that while the language of the narrative is adapted to the appearance assumed by the tempter, it is `That old serpent, called the devil, and Satan, which deceiveth the whole world' (Re 12:9), that is said to be so subtle" - and who is alone cursed by God.[18]

The historicity of the story is not in question here, but simply the manner in which it should be read and understood. As Derek Kidner writes -

"It may still be an open question whether the account transcribes the facts or translates them; that is, whether it is a narrative comparable to such a passage as 2 Sa 11 (which is a straight story of David's sin), or to 2 Sa 12:1-6 (which presents the

---

[17]   Notes on the Book of Genesis; Gall and Inglis, London, 1877, pg. 32/33.

[18]   Ibid.

same event translated into quite other terms that interpret it)."[19]

And on the curse pronounced by God, Kidner writes -

"These words do not imply that hitherto serpents had not been reptiles ... but that the crawling is henceforth symbolic (Is 65:25) - just as in 9:13 a new significance, not a new existence, will be decreed for the rainbow."[20]

The problem facing interpreters is that the story of the Fall represents a very primitive source, one handed across the generations from the dawn of history. Who can now be sure how the ancient narrator wanted his words to be understood? The story also appears to be part poetry, part prose, partly literal and partly figurative. It represents an actual event that happened long ago - the fall of our first parents from innocence into sin, and the words of promise and of penalty spoken by God - but just what literary form the story uses is impossible to determine.

Personally, I prefer to read the story as fact told in a form that is largely poetical and symbolic - that is, I think the narrator used the image of a snake as a literary device to symbolise Satan, without intending to condemn all members of the reptilian class - but I have no argument with those who choose a more literal reading.

James Inglis is wise -

"The difficulties of the subject must suggest to all thoughtful inquirers the necessity of caution in pronouncing dogmatically on what is so imperfectly revealed. The two facts are very clearly set forth,

[19] Tyndale OT Commentaries, Vol One, Genesis; The Tyndale Press, London, 1968, pg. 66.

[20] Ibid. pg. 70.

that our first parents were tempted and fell, and that it was through the devil they were tempted."[21]

And to show that these are not recent perplexities, here is a passage from Irenaeus, the great second century bishop of Lyons -

"How is it possible to say that the serpent, created by God dumb and irrational, was endowed with reason and speech? For if it had the power of itself to speak, to discern, to understand, and to reply to what was spoken by the woman, there would have been nothing to prevent every serpent from doing this also ... Neither was it possible for the evil demon to impart speech to a speechless nature, and thus from that which is not to produce that which is; for if that were the case, he never would have ceased (with the view of leading men astray) from conferring with and deceiving them by means of serpents, and beasts, and birds."[22]

C. THE WORDS OF CHRIST

Jesus summed up the biblical doctrine of Satan in one pungent saying -

You are of your father the devil, and your will is to do your father's desires. He was a murderer from the beginning, and has nothing to do with the truth, because there is no truth in him. When he lies, he

---

[21] Op. cit. pg. 33. For more detailed discussion on The Fall, the student should refer to various commentaries on Genesis, and also to the relevant articles in Bible dictionaries and encyclopedias.

[22] From a lost writing of Irenaeus, cited in the 7th century by Anastasius. Some doubt that the fragment actually comes from the pen of Irenaeus. In any case, it is very ancient. Ante-Nicene Fathers, Vol One; Eerdman's Publishing Co, Grand Rapids, Michigan; 1979 reprint of an 1885 work.

speaks according to his own nature, for he is a liar and the father of lies (Jn 8:44).

Hendriksen comments -

> "(It) is clearly evident from this entire passage, Jesus believes that the devil actually exists, and that he exerts a tremendous influence on earth. To our Lord the prince of evil was not a figment of the imagination, but a grim reality!"[23]

Christ said that the devil was a murderer "from the beginning". Does that mean from the beginning of creation, from the beginning of Satan's existence, or some other "beginning"?

It cannot mean "from the beginning of creation", nor "from the beginning of Satan's existence", because it is axiomatic in scripture that everything made by God in the beginning was "good" - perfect and without trace of sin or corruption -

Death was not God's doing, he takes no pleasure in the extinction of the living. To be - for this he created all; the world's created things have health in them, in them no fatal poison can be found (Wis 1:14; Jerusalem Bible; and cp. also Ge 1:4,10,12,18, 21,25,31).

Since everything created by God was "good" and since Satan is unquestionably one of God's creatures (not some kind of rival deity), it follows that Satan also, at the time of his creation was "good" - he was not at that time a "murderer". At that time, truth was in him, and he had not yet become by nature "a liar, and the father of lies". He was not yet "Satan", the Adversary of God and man.

---

[23]   William Hendriksen, New Testament Commentary, "The Gospel of John"; Baker Book House, Grand Rapids, Michigan, 1953, pg. 61.

When did he become malignant? According to Christ, his initial crime, the cause of his fall, was an act of murder surrounded by lies. In other words, "the beginning" of Satan's sin, was also the beginning of man's. The decisive moment for the devil came when he forsook his true identity, assumed the form of the serpent, and resolved to entice man into rebellion against God. This was an act of "murder", for by persuading Adam and Eve to believe his lie, he caused their death, spiritually and (eventually) physically.

It is not possible to prove that the fall of Satan and man occurred concurrently, but since scripture says nothing to the contrary, it seems to be a fair inference -

> "(This) hypothesis that the fall of Satan and the fall of man took place almost simultaneously is ... substantiated by the fact that both were penally cursed at the same time" (Ge 3:14-17).[24]

If the devil had sinned before that day when he met the woman in the Garden, he would already have been under the doom of God, and probably would not have been so easily able to tempt Eve.

However, other commentators hold that the fall of Satan took place long before the creation of man -

> "(The phrase `from the beginning') more probably (means) at the beginning of the history of salvation, at the dawn of creation, before man had been made. From that time, therefore, Satan had nothing to do with `the truth'."[25]

On this matter of Satan's encounter with truth, Christ makes three accusations –

---

[24]   Payne, op. cit. pg. 294.

[25]   Bauer op. cit. pg. 809.

1. "The truth is not in him"

The "truth" spoken about here is not knowledge of certain facts about the physical universe, but rather that deeper knowledge about the true nature of God and about his role as Creator, Father, and Lord. This deeper truth comes into existence in a rational mind in two stages: first, there is a passive, or neutral, reception of the facts about God; second, there must be a spiritual revelation of these facts; a relationship must be established with them; there must be an inner joyful response to the truth that God represents.

The second part of that appreciation of the truth was rejected by Satan. Before his fall the truth must have been in him in the neutral sense; he must have had at least some awareness of the existence and nature of God, and of his own nature as a creature. But he rejected that truth; he did not permit the Spirit of God to reveal the truth to him in the depths of his spiritual being; he declined the grace of God; he refused to allow the Lord to open the eyes of his understanding. The result? He became possessed by a lie.

Just as we must "learn" the truth through yielding to the persuasion of the Spirit and the working of God's grace in our lives, so did Satan. Just as the truth lies fallow and unproductive in us until it is quickened by an act of divine revelation, so it was in Satan. Just as we may harden our hearts against the truth, refusing to receive it, and so be given over to error and deception, so was Satan (cp. Ep 1:16-18; Cl 1:9- 10; Jn 8:32; 16:13; 17:17; Ro 1:25; 2 Th 2:10-13).

2. "He has nothing to do with the truth"

The inevitable result of the rejection of truth, which is the truth about God, is loss of the truth about oneself. Those who ignore the Creator lose all understanding of themselves as creatures. They become puffed up with pride; they arrogantly imagine themselves to be at least the equals of God, to have a right of independent action, to be answerable to nothing save their own will. Thus they become utterly lost to the truth and enmeshed in a chaos of lies, totally deceived about their real powers, their origins, their destiny.

They begin to imagine that not even the Almighty (if they acknowledge his existence) can hinder their progress in evil.

The king of Babylon received this indictment -

> *You said in your heart, `I will ascend to heaven; above the stars of God I will set my throne on high ... I will ascend above the heights of the clouds, I will make myself like the Most High.' But you are brought down to Sheol, to the depths of the Pit" (Is 14:13-15).*

Also the king of Tyre -

> *Because your heart is proud, and you have said, `I am a god, I sit in the seat of the gods, in the heart of the seas,' yet you are but a man, and no god, though you consider yourself as wise as a god ... therefore, behold, I will bring strangers upon you, the most terrible of the nations .. . Will you still say, `I am a god,' in the presence of those who slay you?" (Ez 28:2-9).*

Thus the devil, having scorned the truth the Father was willing to reveal to him, now has "nothing to do with the truth" - for him, truth is inaccessible, loathsome, a thing to oppose bitterly. He has lost all capacity to receive the truth. God has condemned him to believe a lie, thinking it to be true. The same dread penalty awaits all who walk in his steps.

3.   "He speaks lies according to his own nature"

It is endemic among those who have perverted the truth and embraced falsehood, to impose their darkness on all they meet. Even if they should happen to speak words that are true, they do so for corrupt ends and within a context of rebellion against God. So the devil may "appear as an angel of light", but he cannot deny his own real nature. The lie he represents is easily discovered behind the camouflage (2 Co 11:14; and cp. also Mt 4:5-7; Mk 1:34; 3:11-12; Ac 16:16-18).

"(Satan) willed to be sufficient to himself, persisted in his blind complacency in his own nature and thereby lost his true value, his office, his rank, perverted his nature to lying, and so became the `father of lies' who `exchanged the truth about God for a lie' (Ro 1:25). So completely did he become the champion and protagonist of lying that between it and him complete identity was achieved. `Everywhere where lying has become a principle of life, a principle of understanding, of willing, of acting, there Satan is directly at work' (A. Mager)."[26]

Acceptance of these lies by the human race has made Satan the prince and god of this world - Jn 12:31; 14:30; 2 Co 4:4; Ep 2:2, and has given him the power of death (He 2:14).

II. BABYLON AND TYRE

Here are some mysteries: the original identity of Satan; whether he was a seraph, cherub, archangel, or another kind of being altogether; the time of his creation; the time of his fall; his name - these matters are all shrouded in darkness. Very little, if any, clear information is given in scripture.

Some commentators, however, see a reference to the fall of Satan in Is 14:4-23 and in Ez 28:1-19. From those passages they argue: that Satan began as a magnificent angel, belonging to the class of cherubim (Ez 28:14); that he was radiantly beautiful (vs. 12-13), holy (vs. 15), full of wisdom (vs. 3-5), immensely powerful (Is.

---

[26] Myriam Prager, in Bauer, op. cit. pg. 811.

14:16); and that he was named after the lovely morning star, Lucifer (vs. 12).[27]

Geoffrey Chaucer (died 1400) shared with his contemporaries the notion that Satan was a fallen angel named Lucifer -

> With Lucifer, although an angel he
> And not a man, I purpose to begin.
> For notwithstanding angels cannot be
> The sport of Fortune, yet he fell through sin
> Down into hell, and he is yet therein.
> O Lucifer, brightest of angels all,
> Now thou art Satan, and canst never win
> Out of thy miseries; how great thy fall![28]

The basic sin of Lucifer is said to have been pride, attempting to usurp the position and prerogatives of deity.

---

[27] The RSV reads, "*How are you fallen from heaven, O Day Star, son of Dawn!*" The KJV reads, "*How art thou fallen from heaven, O Lucifer, son of the morning!*" The allusion is actually to "the morning star", the planet Venus. "Lucifer" is the Latin name of this star.

Because of a belief that Isaiah intended his prophecy to transcend its local political setting, and to describe the pride and ruin of Satan, "Lucifer" was early taken to be Satan's personal name –

> "Unhappy spirits that fell with Lucifer,
> Conspired against our God with Lucifer,
> And are damned forever with Lucifer" - *Marlow.*

> "Lucifer ... brighter once amid the host
> Of angels, than that star the stars among"-.*Milton*

The translation of the Latin word into the English of the KJV greatly enhanced the use of Lucifer (almost certainly wrongly) as a proper noun for the devil.

[28] Canterbury Tales, "*The Monk's Tale*;" tr. by Nevill Coghill; Penguin Classics, 1982; pg. 207.

A. "LUCIFER" AND THE DEVIL

Leo Harris writes -

"Here (Ez 28:1-19) the prophecy is addressed primarily to the 'Prince of Tyrus', and yet, as we examine the words of the prophet more closely, it becomes obvious to us that he is using language which could only apply to Satan as the unseen power behind the Prince of Tyrus ... The references (in vs. 2, 13-16) are obviously to someone other than the Prince of Tyrus. They direct our attention to the real power behind this earthly ruler. They describe Satan as a creature of great beauty and holiness who enjoyed the confidence and favour of God, 'till iniquity was found in thee.'

"Isaiah 14:1-23 ... is another case of a prophet identifying the real power behind an earthly ruler - this time the king of Babylon. Isaiah foretells the judgments about to befall the king of Babylon, but then in verses 12-14 we see an obvious reference to Satan, called Lucifer. It is Satan who expresses his own spirit through such men, thus causing them to exalt themselves as he sought to exalt himself, to rebel against God as he rebelled against God, only to be cast down as he was cast down. Only Satan and those inspired by Satan could be capable of such arrogance and pride as expressed in (the words of vs. 1 ... It is believed that there were originally three archangels, Michael, Gabriel, and Lucifer, each having command over one-third of the angels of God. There are certain indications in scripture that Lucifer's authority at least equalled that of the archangel Michael."[29]

Among those who hold to the above view, the suggestion is sometimes made that Michael was in a special sense linked with the Father, Gabriel with the Holy Spirit, and Lucifer with the Son; and that this link between Lucifer and Christ is one of the reasons Jesus took on human form - to undo the awful harm brought upon humanity by the rebellion of his personal archangel. But that is all supposition, without biblical support.

Many evangelical authors, particularly those writing or preaching at a popular level, endorse this linking of the kings of Tyre and Babylon, and of Lucifer, with the devil. But there are many other commentators who hold to

B. A CONTRARY VIEW

These commentators fall into three groups -

1. Those who allow that Satan is the key figure in Is 14:12-15, but not in Ez 28:13-15. J. Barton Payne is one of these, and about the Ezekiel passage he writes -

> " ... the presence of the precious stones and gold, and the fact that the subject was created in connection with the garden of Eden, suggests Adam (Ge 2:7,12), and not Satan; while in Ez 28:14 the reference to the mountain of God and to the cherub covering (the ark) suggests the Temple on Mt. Zion, but not the pride of the devil. There thus appears to be no biblical basis for assuming from Ex 28:14 that Satan was once a member of the class of the cherubim."[30]

---

[29])Victory Over Satan, Crusade Publications, Adelaide, 1976, pg. 10-12.
[30] Op. cit. pg. 294, 295.

However, a large number of interpreters would say that the arguments Payne uses to dismiss Satan from Ez 28, just as readily dismiss him from Is 14. So we find another body of opinion-

2. Those who claim it is quite inappropriate to read into either passage an allusion (under the symbol of earthly monarchs) to the fall of Satan. Thus Keil and Delitzsch comment (on Is 14:12-13) -

> "Lucifer, as a name given to the devil, was derived from this passage, which the fathers ... interpreted, without any warrant whatever, as relating to the apostasy and punishment of the angelic leaders. The appellation is a perfectly appropriate one for the king of Babel, on account of the early date of the Babylonian culture, which reached back as far as the grey twilight of primeval times, and also because of its predominant astrological character."[31]

Keil and Delitzsch are rather blunt. They claim there is "no warrant whatever" for writing Satan into Is 14 and Ez 28, and they quite remove the devil from their explanation of the oracles of the two prophets. But Keil and Delitzsch do at least draw attention to an ancient identification of the King of Tyre with "Lucifer". A great many notable commentators do not give the theory even that much attention. They ignore it completely! They apply the two oracles exclusively to the natural monarchs of Babylon and Tyre, finding it unnecessary to introduce a supernatural element in order to interpret the prophecies.

3. Perhaps a fair opinion would be to allow that the prophets intended to describe only earthly kings, and not the devil; yet since the princes of Babylon and Tyre served Satan, not God,

---

[31]   Op. cit. Vol.7, Isaiah, pg. 312.

they behaved in a manner true to their Lord's character. So their rise and fall followed the pattern of their master's rise and fall.

That is a universal principle, as Jesus suggested when he accused the Pharisees -

> *You do what you have heard from your father ...*
> *You do what your father did ... You are of your*
> *father the devil, and your will is to do your father's*
> *desires" (Jn 8:38,41,44).*

That is why the drama of the devil's proud rebellion against God, and his inevitable downfall, are perpetually repeated by all who exalt themselves as he did. In this sense, the ruin of the kings of Babylon and Tyre are earthly examples of a greater havoc that took place long before in the heavenly realm. They were repetitions in a smaller theatre of the stages in Satan's downfall.

If what I am saying is true, then scripture gives no direct description of the origin, identity, or fall of Satan. The "beginning" of the biblical revelation is found in Ge 3, and at that point the devil has already assumed the character of murderer and liar. Whoever adds to that description is speaking from conjecture.

III. SATAN'S SIN

(A bishop) must not be a recent convert, or he may be puffed up with conceit and fall into the condemnation of the devil" ... "The angels that did not keep their own position but left their proper dwelling have been kept by him in eternal chains ... just as Sodom and Gomorrah ... in like manner these men in their dreamings defile the flesh, reject authority, and revile the glorious ones ... they walk in the way of Cain, and abandon themselves for the sake of gain to Balaam's error, and perish in Korah's rebellion (1 Ti 3:6; Jude 6-11).

Those two passages give an insight into the causes of the fall of Satan and of the angels that were cast out of heaven with him.

Albert Barnes comments on 1 Ti 3:6 -

> "It is here intimated that the cause of the apostasy of
> Satan was pride - a cause which is as likely to have
> been the true one as any other. Who can tell but it
> may have been produced by some new honour
> which was conferred upon him in heaven, and that
> his virtue was not found sufficient for the untried
> circumstances in which he was placed? Much of the
> apostasy from eminent virtue in this world, arises
> from this cause; and possibly the case of Satan may
> have been the most signal instance of this kind
> which has occurred in the universe."[32]

Barnes suggests that the devil's foremost sin may have been an
arrogant conceit, caused by his unexpected elevation to a position
of exalted power and authority. That may well have been the case;
but remember that scripture does not specify the nature of Satan's
pride - it simply avers that he was (or became) proud, and that this
was the chief cause of his banishment from heaven.

But sin never stands alone. One corruption leads to another.
Iniquity multiplies itself. So Jude details four other aspects of the
devils' fall -

A. SELF-WILL

He did not keep his own position, but left his proper dwelling. This
was a denial of the Father's right to assign a place and a task to all
his creatures; it was an act of self-will in opposition to the will of
God; it was an assertion of personal desire against the purpose of
God. All such refusal to submit to the sovereignty of God must
result in divine judgment: "kept by God in eternal chains in the
nether gloom until the judgment of the great day."

---

[32]   Op. cit. pg. 1140

A question arises here: if Satan and the fallen angels are chained "in nether gloom", how is it they can still roam the earth, tempting and tormenting mankind? Peter presents us with the same problem (2 Pe 2:4) -

> *God did not spare the angels when they sinned, but cast them into hell and committed them to pits of nether gloom to be kept until the judgment.*

Commenting on the latter passage, Barnes writes -

> "This representation that the mass of fallen angels are confined in `Tartarus', or in hell, is not inconsistent with the representations which elsewhere occur that their leader is permitted to roam the earth, and that even many of those spirits are allowed to tempt men. It may still be true that the mass are confined within the limits of their dark abode; and it may even be true also that Satan and those who are permitted to roam the earth are under bondage, and are permitted to range only within certain bounds, and that they are so secured that they will be brought to trial at the last day."[33]

Lu 8:31 seems to imply that the dread depths of "the Abyss" irrevocably imprison some demons, while others are still, for the time being, permitted to traverse the earth.

There is another view. In contrast with the splendours of heaven, this earth must seem to the angels as a "pit of nether gloom". To be confined to this planet until the day of final judgment may be a bleak existence for the fallen angels. But there is a problem: the earth is nowhere else described as a place of punishment for angels. Further, when we remember that the earth is still the dwelling-place of the church, and the holy angels are constantly

---

[33]   Op. cit. pg. 1450.

passing between earth and heaven, to portray this beautiful planet as "hell" seems grotesque.

The meaning of the word translated "hell" (Tartarus) seems to preclude its application to the earth. Tartarus does not occur anywhere else in the Bible, so we must glean its meaning from its use in other Greek literature. Homer, in the Iliad, describes Tartarus as a place beneath the earth, as far below Hades as Heaven is above the earth, and closed by iron gates. Although later poets used the name as almost synonymous with Hades, it nonetheless retained the idea of the deepest part of hell, the uttermost nether regions, the darkest, coldest, pit.

> Hesiod and Plato expressed a similar view, and Hesychius described Tartarus as "the lowest place beneath the earth." Heracles descended from the earth's surface into Tartarus to defy Pluto and to capture Cerberus, the dreaded three-headed dog. Tartarus was also the place of deep darkness in which Zeus confined the defeated Titans.[34]

That latter myth parallels the idea expressed by Peter; the Greeks thought of Tartarus as a place of punishment for the angels. It is uncertain how much of the Greek concept Peter endorsed. Perhaps he was simply using the Greek myth as an illustration of the certain and final punishment God will inflict upon the fallen angels. Perhaps, while rejecting the mythical accretions, he accepted the existence of a place where God has confined the fallen angels, and saw that it was similar enough to Tartarus to warrant the same name.

In any case, we know that Satan, and the angels who fell with him, are already imprisoned, and already writhing under punishment; yet they are not confined enough to prevent them from continuing

---

[34]   Information from Smith's Classical Dictionary, and from Bengel.

their warfare against earth and heaven. Their condemnation is not yet complete; their cup of iniquity is not yet full. But nothing can prevent that final hour, the great day of God's judgment, when they will stand before the throne and hear the appalling sentence of doom.

B. UNNATURAL LUST

Though called upon to perfect his moral character (cp. He 5:8) by choosing to emulate the righteousness of the Lord God, Satan perverted holiness into immorality by acting with unnatural lust. That is, had he remained true to the pure nature given him by God, he would naturally have desired obedience, humility, and truth; but he chose instead to stir up unnatural desire, to act against his proper nature, and to stifle every inclination toward doing the will of God. His lust, his immorality; was not of the flesh but of the spirit, hence it became utterly depraved, relentlessly corrupt, and beyond reclamation. Sodom and Gomorrah are an example both of the sin of Satan, and of the doom awaiting him: "a punishment of eternal fire."

C. REJECTING TRUTH

Jude talks about those "dreamers (who) defile the flesh, reject authority, and revile the glorious ones." He is referring to people who are a law to themselves, who live by personal revelation, who acknowledge no truth except what they themselves choose to believe. They follow the example of the angels who allowed their own deceit to delude them into thinking they were wiser than God.

Thus the Serpent drew Eve to question the Divine wisdom. All who reject the truth must believe a lie, and eat the bitter fruits of their own wilful ignorance. Thoroughly defiled by their lies they reject all lawful authority, and give themselves to cursing instead of blessing. Jude saw the primeval sin of Satan flowering again in these crazed "dreamers" with their godless revelations.

Most commentators allow that the heretics referred to by both Jude and Peter, were those groups known as "Gnostics" (from the

Greek, *gnosis* = knowledge). Broadly, the gnostics claimed a special knowledge, based on special revelations or secret sources, which alone provided the key to salvation. Knowledge of Christ and the scriptures alone was insufficient. Christ could be understood only in the context of the hidden knowledge owned by the gnostic.

Michael Green writes -

> "Clearly we have here in Jude the early signs of the specific Gnostic systems which were to plague the subapostolic Church. Claims to special `knowledge' made men indifferent to the demands of morality (you were, after all, saved by `gnosis', not by behaviour), indifferent to the needs of their brethren (it was essentially personal illumination and this made you feel superior to the common herd), indifferent, too, to the dicta of church leaders (for, after all, it was you, not they, who had `arrived'). Those who lay claim to direct, immediate knowledge of the Almighty's mind commonly fall into the same errors today."[35]

Whenever you find people claiming special or unique revelation, knowledge which is not generally accessible to the people of God, or which makes them scornful of spiritual authority, or disobedient to scripture, then you see a replica of one of Satan's original sins.

D. CAIN, BALAAM, AND KORAH

The devil's servants endlessly repeat the sins of their master, and in so doing expose the way Satan fell. Jude shows three parts to this -

- ♦ they walk in the way of Cain

---

[35]   Tyndale New Testament Commentaries, 2 Peter; in loc.; The Tyndale Press, London, 1968.

- they abandon themselves to Balaam's error

- they perish in Korah's rebellion

What is the way of Cain? This person is governed by hate instead of love, resentful of any honour given to another, ruled by envy and malice. And what is that but murder? For "anyone who hates his brother is a murderer, and you know that no murderer has eternal life abiding in him" (1 Jn 3:15). The devil denied love and affirmed hate. So Jesus called him "a murderer from the beginning" (Jn 8:44).

It is inevitable that those who walk in the way of Cain, selfish, egotistical, careless of their neighbour, soon abandon themselves to Balaam's error - that is, to the pursuit at any cost of material riches. All their happiness is located in earthly possessions. Their only wealth consists of things that can be seen, touched, or tasted. They have no eyes for the invisible things of God that alone abide forever.

So Satan, true to his corrupted form, and judging Christ by his own perverted idea of riches, thought he could tempt Jesus by offering him "all the kingdoms of the world and the glory of them". The devil completely failed to understand how pitiful and absurd such a temptation must have seemed to Jesus, as it has since done to countless other godly souls who have eagerly chosen "to share ill-treatment with the people of God rather than to enjoy the fleeting pleasures of sin", and who have "considered abuse suffered for the Christ greater wealth than the treasures of Egypt" (He 11:25,26; and cp. also vs. 13-16).

It has ever been the thought of the world, aping its satanic lord, that "every man has his price", that every man is brother to Balaam, willing to sell his soul for the sake of gain. But the godly remember the shameful end to which Balaam's error brought him (Nu 31:8); they reject the devil's falsehood, and they adhere to the vision of God.

Only one ends awaits those who walk in Cain's way and abandon themselves to Balaam's error: they will perish (as Satan perished) in Korah's rebellion. How can it be other than insane for any creature to spawn a revolt against the Creator? Yet that is the inescapable folly of all who refuse to love the truth. For all who love a lie the salvation of God will forever remain unknown.

Upon Satan, and upon all who embrace his error, "God sends a strong delusion, to make them believe what is false, so that all may be condemned who did not believe the truth but had pleasure in unrighteousness" (2 Th 2:9-12). And what is this "strong delusion"? Simply, to believe this lie: "I can successfully defy the Almighty!" In swelling hubris Satan and his minions, demon and human, vainly imagine they can with impunity afflict the saints and ravage the kingdom of God.

But as surely as Satan already feels the dread chill of Tartarus enveloping him, and as surely as Korah and his followers were cast into the abyss (Nu 16:31-35), so surely will all those perish who rebel against either the immediate or delegated authority of God.[36]

IV.MORAL, SPIRITUAL, AND INTELLECTUAL RUIN

What I have said so far shows three parts to the fall of Satan: moral, spiritual, and intellectual. In all three there is rebellion against the natural order established by God:

[36] Note that Korah pretended that his revolt was not against God, but only against what he claimed was dictatorship by Moses and Aaron. However, since Moses possessed delegated authority from God, the Lord judged Korah as rebelling against himself, and punished him accordingly. To resist divinely delegated authority, whether in scripture, the church, the home, or in the world, is to resist God himself

- ◆ Satan offended moral order by choosing unnatural lust in place of purity - he coveted those things he should have avoided, and spurned those things he should have desired.

- ◆ he offended spiritual order by exalting himself above the will of God, thus worshipping the creature instead of the Creator. He is still ruled by self-adulation, and even now is scarcely terrified of the coming wrath.

- ◆ he offended intellectual order by refusing to acknowledge the need for his creaturely intelligence to be completed by obedience to God.

The Lord has so constructed both angels and men that they must remain forever incomplete, their potential unrealised, unless they seek fruition and fulfilment through loving service of God and of each other. It is the vanity alike of fallen angels and men to imagine they have no need of the Divine touch upon their lives. Thus they sin against their own true nature, and against the proper order of things. They become outcasts in God's universe.

CHAPTER THREE

OUR REDEMPTION

How do you picture your salvation? Scripture portrays it as a mighty struggle between a strong man and one who is stronger -

When a strong man, fully armed, guards his own palace, his goods are in peace; but when one stronger than he assails him and overcomes him, he takes his armour in which he trusted, and divides his spoil (Lu 11:21-22; also Mt 12:29; Mk 3:27).

The strong man is Satan; the stronger man is Christ. This brief parable shows several things about our relationship to the kingdom of darkness -

♦ first, Jesus does not hesitate to describe Satan as "strong" - he is a powerful adversary, even against Christ. The analogy is not one of weakness opposing strength, but rather of the strong opposing the stronger. To defeat this strong man required supreme sacrifice from the stronger man. Though now defeated, Satan still has great strength. We need not fear him; but we must respect him (not even the archangel Michael presumed to "pronounce a reviling judgment upon him", Jude 9).

♦ second, though Christ (at Calvary) tore away his armour, and divided the spoils of the kingdom of darkness, Satan is still able to afflict the people of God, and his armies are still waging war against the armies of heaven.

♦ third, Christ has "assailed and overcome" the devil. That divine triumph has created a basis, in all our conflicts with the enemy, upon which we may build continuous personal victory. Those who ally themselves with the strong man will be defeated by the stronger; those who ally themselves with the stronger man will defeat the strong!

♦ fourth, the parable suggests the immense mystery that surrounds heaven's war with hell. Why must the victory of righteousness over unrighteousness be so hardly won? Why was the cost of victory so immense?

Satan was willing to pay "all the kingdoms of the earth, and their glory" (Mt 4:8-9); but Christ prevailed, because he was willing to offer his own life - a price of infinitely greater value (Jn 10:11). Yet to us the cost still seems too high, and we wonder why victory could not have been bought more cheaply.

Then there is the mystery of the continuance of the conflict. Jesus spoke this parable after casting a demon out of a dumb man. That man himself was the "palace" Satan had formerly occupied in "peace".

To dispossess the devil, and to set the man free, may have appeared outwardly to require little more than a few words of command. But inwardly, in the spiritual realm, a fierce conflict was taking place - the stronger man was assailing the strong man, and overcoming him only at great cost.

That same war is still being fought whenever the servants of God seek to liberate enemy occupied "territory".

Some aspects of these mysteries may never be fully understood by the church. But other things have been clearly told us - primarily, that Christ's triumph is absolute, and that our victory is guaranteed. These are the ideas explored in this chapter.

I. THE STRENGTHS AND WEAKNESSES OF OUR FOE

A. THE STRENGTHS OF SATAN

1. He Has Authority

Satan rules "the kingdoms of the world," and may dispose of them as he pleases (Mt 4:8-9; Lu 4:5-6; 1 Jn 5:19, "The whole world is in the power of the evil one.")

Notice how Jesus did not dispute the devil's claim that he could give Christ "all the kingdoms of the world." Nor did Jesus argue with the assertion that "all this authority and their glory" had been "delivered" to the devil, and his boast, "I can give it to whom I will."

God has never surrendered his right to raise or crush nations according to his own sovereign will (Je 1:10; 18:1-10; etc); nonetheless, it is generally true that the nations of this world lie in the grip of Satan; wickedness, not righteousness, governs them. Possession of the kingdoms of the world, of all their authority, all their glory, all their wealth, conveys to the devil vast spiritual and material strength. He is indeed a powerful foe!

2. He Is "The God Of This World"

Because they give him worship, Satan has gained power "to bind the minds of the unbelievers", to "veil the eyes of those who are perishing", and so "to keep them from seeing the light of the gospel of the glory of Christ" (2 Co 4:3-4).

3. He Is "The Prince Of The Power Of The Air"

That unusual expression puzzles commentators. They give different translations, they understand it in different ways. Some of the variations are -

♦ the ruler of the spiritual powers in space;

- the ruler of the kingdom of the air;

- the evil ruler of the spiritual realm;

- the commander of the spiritual powers of the air;

- the powerful prince of the air;

- the prince of the aerial powers;

- the Ruler of the Kingdom of the Lower Air.

The expression is usually understood in one of three ways -

a. Paul reveals his belief (shared by most of his contemporaries) that the atmospheric heavens are the particular habitation of demons, so that we are constantly surrounded by a thick mass of evil spirits who seek every opportunity to do us harm. Satan is the king of this wicked host. Unbelievers are especially subject to control by these demonic agents; but Christ has delivered his church from their power.

b. Other commentators do not agree that Paul accepted the prevailing Jewish superstitions about the "air" being the habitation of innumerable demons. They argue that Paul used the word "air" in this passage, not in its literal sense, but figuratively, to signify the spiritual dimension. As though he were saying that the sinful world is governed by a mighty prince (Satan), who exercises real power, but whose form of existence is not physical, but spiritual.

c. Others, while they agree that Paul was not endorsing the current notion of the air being peculiarly the abode of evil spirits, nonetheless cannot agree that the statement should not be taken literally. So Hendriksen writes -

"This passage, in conjunction with others (3:10,15; 6:12), clearly teaches that God has tenanted the supermundane realm with innumerable hosts, and that in its lower regions the minions of Satan are engaged in their destructive missions."[37]

The general idea here is that because of rebellion and sin the present world has become subject to oppression by the kingdom of darkness. Demonic powers move about the earth, through the air, encouraging opposition to God, seeking to afflict the church, warring against the purposes of God. The "air" itself does not belong to Satan, nor does he have any more control over it than he does over any other part of the physical creation. But Paul uses the phrase "power of the air" to suggest the global nature, the cosmic proportions, of the titanic spiritual struggle that is being endlessly waged between the forces of good and evil.

Paul gives a three-fold description of the force against which we must contend -

♦ it governs the course of this world;

♦ it rules in the heavens around us;

♦ it works in wicked men.

Those things expose the source of the devil's strength -

♦ the fallen world gladly follows the program laid down by Satan;

♦ it submits to the rule of darkness (the word "air" in the ancient mythology sometimes held the sense of "darkness", of fog, chill, and gloom, in contrast with "light");

♦ and "the sons of disobedience" yield themselves willingly to the working of a satanic spirit.

♦ The church opposes each of those aspects of the devil's power -

---

[37]   Op. cit. Ephesians in. loc.

♦ we do not follow his course, but the ways of God;

♦ we have escaped his malign aerial influence, and are governed by the benign providence of God;

♦ we spurn the spirit that works disobedience, and we offer to God the obedience of sons.

Thus for us, all the strength of Satan is nullified. And all this takes place right in the heart of what Satan always thought was his own territory! (Jn 12:31; 14:30). It is not surprising that he wars against the church with unflagging hate.

Leo Harris writes -

> "The church could be called God's secret weapon.
> With Israel scattered abroad and Christ in the tomb,
> Satan may well have considered himself the victor.
> But then God raised his Son from the dead, received
> him back into heaven, sent forth the Holy Spirit,
> and brought into being the church ... It could well
> be that God purposely withheld any specific
> reference in the OT to either the resurrection of
> Christ or the calling out of the church. Satan, not
> possessing omniscience, or all-knowingness, was
> taken by surprise when God chose the church to be
> the instrument in his hand, to enforce the victory of
> Calvary, and overcome all the works of the devil ...
> However, it is for this very reason that Satan and his
> demons make every active Christian, as well as the
> Spirit-filled church in general, the target for their
> hostile activities during this dispensation."[38]

Christ has "delivered us from the dominion of darkness", but that kingdom itself has not ceased to exist. Its dominion is still world-

---

[38]   Op. cit. pg. 23, 24.

wide; its princes and hierarchies are flourishing; its slaves are multitudinous; its armies are not yet vanquished; its strongholds still resist the attacks of the saints and of the holy angels (cp. 2 Co 10:4).

How tragic this intertwining with human affairs of the dark kingdom! Its invidious influence permeates every facet of life outside of the church, and even manages from time to time to invade the very house of God. For so long as this kingdom remains intact, the power of Satan over men will wax bitter and strong.

4. He Is The "Destroyer"

Satan has power to "destroy the flesh" (1 Co 5:3-5; 1 Ti 1:20) The inference in these passages is that the church provides a covering for its members. For as long as believers remain in close fellowship with the church they are inviolable to Satan's attacks. But if they leave the church, or are cast out from it, then they may become susceptible to the worst malice of Satan (cp. 1 Co 11:30; Ac 5:1-11; Ps 109:6 ff). I do not mean that every such person will be so afflicted, but Satan has the right and power to afflict them if he chooses, or if God allows.

Those verses state that the devil has the ability to inflict physical disease, or other kinds of deprivation and suffering, upon the "flesh" of those who are cut off from Divine protection.

5. He Is "Like A Roaring Lion"

Behold him prowling around, seeking someone to devour! (1 Pe 5:8). This vivid metaphor conveys a clear impression of vast malice, huge strength, tireless cunning, effortless pursuit of seemingly helpless prey. Despite the dread wound he received at the cross, Satan retains enormous energy. His force is scarcely abated. Without Christ, we would be defenceless as gazelles under the claws of this fierce predator.

By Christ and Christ alone we hope to prevail.

6.   He Holds The Power Of Death

See He 2:14-15. Satan does not have power to inflict death merely by his own will. Nonetheless, he does seek by the fear of death to keep men under his dominion. By his instigation death came into human experience through sin - "it was the devil's envy that brought death into the world, as those who are his partners will discover" (Wis 2:24; Ro 5:12).

What sustains the devil's power? Simply this mysterious association with death, both physical and spiritual. Hence, scripture shows that the devil's disruptive influence will not be finally annihilated until death also is obliterated. Satan and Death move reluctantly toward destruction on the same day. The cessation of death will mean the end of Satan's power. He gained power by using death; he will lose it when the link between himself and death is finally broken –

The devil who had deceived them was thrown into the lake of fire and brimstone ... Then Death and Hades were thrown into the lake of fire ... and death shall be no more ... " (Re 20:10,14; 21:4).

B. THE LIMITATIONS OF SATAN

You should firmly understand the strict limits placed on the devil's ability to exert his power and inflict his works. He does not have unfettered liberty nor unrestricted power. He cannot go anywhere or do anything he pleases. Two impervious frontiers confine him -

♦   the boundaries of his own finite nature;

♦   the boundaries of the will of God.

It is just as impossible for the devil as it is for man to go beyond the limits of his own being. Satan is a creature of God. He has no choice but to exist within the definition of his nature established when he was given life. He cannot do more than God has created him to do. Nor can he do more than God permits him to do. He remains forever unable to breach the will of God, and is just as much bound as the rest of the creation to submit to heaven's rule. It is finally impossible for the will of the Creator to be successfully resisted by any of his creatures.

♦ Some of the areas in which Satan is finite and limited are given in scripture

♦ he cannot penetrate your secret thoughts; for knowledge of what happens in the private recesses of your mind is a uniquely divine attribute (1 Sa 16:7; Ps 139:2; Pr 15:11; Je 17:9,10). Satan can know only those thoughts, or only that part of your mind you choose to reveal to him.

♦ he cannot influence you, nor inflict upon you anything, beyond what God permits (Jb 1:6-2:9; Re 2:10).

♦ he cannot take away from Christ anyone who is unwilling to go (Jn 10:28; Ro 8:38,39).

♦ he cannot bring pressure of temptation upon any person beyond the limits specified by God (Lu 22:31; 1 Co 10:13).

♦ he cannot resist the knowledge of his own defeat, and he is obliged to yield to those who know their authority in Christ (Ja 4:7; Lu 10:19; Mk 16:17-18).

♦ his intelligence is corrupted, so his understanding of scripture is superficial; he comprehends only as much of the word of God as he has been able to glean from the church (1 Co 2:7-16; Ep 3:10).

♦ he does not know the future, for that also is a uniquely divine attribute (Is 44:7; 46:9,10). He remains as ignorant as we are of the details of God's plan.

♦ he cannot prevent nor reverse the processes of the new birth in a person called by God, who yields to the Holy Spirit (1 Jn 5:18).

♦ he cannot destroy any church that has not first destroyed itself (Mt 16:18).

♦ he cannot prevent the judgments of God from falling upon any of his servants, nor upon himself (Re 20:7-10).

II. THE TOTAL VICTORY OF CHRIST

A. GAINED AT CALVARY

In the passage of scripture that began this chapter (Lu 11:21-22), Christ declared bluntly that

♦ he is stronger than Satan

♦ he has assailed Satan

♦ he has overcome Satan

♦ he has broken Satan's defences

♦ he has plundered the kingdom of darkness.

What an unequivocal assertion of complete victory! Scripture repeats it many times; see for example, Jn 12:31; Cl 1:13; 1 Jn 3:8; etc. The locus of this victory is Calvary. The cross was the specific battle field where Jesus "disarmed the principalities and powers and made a public example of them, and triumphed over them" (Cl 2:15).

Leo Harris reminds us that the victory gained by Christ on the Cross was not gained for his own sake; it was a representative victory, gained on our behalf.[39]

B. A REPRESENTATIVE VICTORY

If Christ had died a natural death as a prophet or a teacher or merely as a good man, his personal authority over Satan would have perished with him. Thank God, he was more than that. Being

---

[39] Leo Harris is the author of the following paragraphs, to the end of section (B) (5).

the sinless Son of God, his vicarious death and triumphant resurrection legally secured authority over Satan for everyone who believes in the efficacy of his substitutionary work.

The victory Christ won in the wilderness temptation was on his own behalf; but the victory he won on Calvary was on our behalf ... Christ utterly conquered the powers of darkness and exposed them as defeated captives over whom he had gloriously triumphed in his death on the cross.

When Jesus died and rose again, he defeated Satan in five realms -

1. Christ conquered Satan as the author of sin

See 1 Jn 3:8; 2 Co 5:21.

2. Christ conquered him as the author of sickness

See Is 53:4. Matthew applies this verse specifically to the healing ministry of Jesus (Mt 8:16- 17). Thus it is seen that Christ bore our sicknesses along with our sins when he suffered on the cross. For this reason he healed the sick as well as forgiving sinners. Sickness as much as sin, is a work of the devil (Ac 10:38).

3. Christ conquered him in the realm of death.

See He 2:14-15. The word "destroy" in this text does not mean to annihilate, but rather to render ineffective or powerless. Christ did not annihilate Satan, but he did strip from him the authority of death.

Death is still in the world, it is still an enemy. But Christ delivers us from the fear of death, for we know he is death's Master. We believe the declaration he made after his resurrection and ascension: "I hold the keys of death and hell!" (Re 1:18).

4. Christ conquered him as ruler of the kingdoms of the world

We saw how that, in the wilderness temptations, Satan offered to Jesus the kingdoms of the world (Mt 4:8-9) ... Jesus did not dispute the fact Satan had a right to offer the kingdoms of this world.

Rather, he knew that the devil was seeking to entice him to bypass the cross and accept world dominion from his hand ...

How we praise God that our Lord did not succumb to this satanic temptation, but was willing to go to Calvary. Now the victory is won - Christ has risen from the dead and is seated at the Father's right hand. One day, and soon, he will come again. Then the prophet will see his words fulfilled -

> *"The kingdoms of this world are become the kingdoms of our Lord, and of his Christ, and he shall reign for ever and ever."(Re 11:15)*

5.   Christ conquered him in the realm of universal dominion - heaven, earth, and under the earth

In Ph 2:5-11 we read of our Lord's self-humiliation, his obedience to the death of the cross, and his exaltation by God the Father ... Verse 10 states, "That at the name of Jesus every knee shall bow, of things in heaven, and things in earth, and things under the earth" ...

Ep 4:8-10 tells a similar story, that Jesus first descended into the lower parts of the earth, then he ascended far above all heavens, and in so doing, "he led captivity captive", or, led a multitude of captives. First to the lowest realm, then to the highest realm, and everywhere he was proclaimed the victor over Satan and his demons and all his evil works.

Thus the victory of Christ on Calvary's cross has defeated Satan in heaven, earth, and under the earth. Christ is now Lord of all! Christ conquered humanity's conquerors. He paid the price for our deliverance. He won the victory in our name that we may appropriate it to the full.

Thank God for the representative victory won by our Lord Jesus Christ.[40]

C. A FREELY AVAILABLE VICTORY

Do you doubt the devil's awareness of the savage defeat Christ has inflicted on him? Then look at the many accounts in the gospels in which a "possessed person clearly reflects the terror, torment, and fury of the defeated devil before the irresistible advance of his conqueror" (Bauer) - see Mt 8:29; Mk 1:24,32; 3:11; 5:7; 9:20; Lu 4:34; 8:28,31.

Thus the scriptures everywhere bid the people of God to rejoice greatly, because "now the salvation and the power and the kingdom of our God and the authority of his Christ have come, for the accuser of our brethren has been thrown down ... and they have conquered him by the blood of the Lamb and by the word of their testimony" (Re 12:10- 11).

The representative victory of Christ over Satan is complete and free for every believer!

But how can these statements about the decisive victory of the cross be reconciled with the experience of the people of God? Often the devil, that roaring lion, that great dragon, that ancient serpent, seems to be far from defeated! The strengths he still has sometimes seem overwhelming, and the resources of the church pitifully feeble. We do indeed find ourselves in the centre of

III. A CONTINUING CONFLICT

Despite the crushing defeat inflicted on Satan at Calvary, it was in a sense only a battle won, not the war. True, the loss of that battle has ensured the devil's final overthrow; but the war continues.

---

[40]   Op. cit. pg. 18-20

Satan still has at his disposal great armies, many weapons, prodigious strength. Many scriptures show the ongoing conflict that constantly embroils us:

- ◆ the evil one is able to snatch away the word from the hearts of those without understanding (Mt 13:19), and he can plant his evil agents in the church itself (vs. 39).

- ◆ Jesus found it necessary to pray that his disciples might be kept from the evil one (Jn 17:15).

- ◆ Satan can deceive people within the church, and fill them with lies (Ac 5:3).

- ◆ he is still able to seize and afflict those who violate the commands of God (1 Co 5:5), and he can tempt those who leave themselves open to his attack (7:5).

- ◆ he can gain advantage over those who are ignorant of his designs, or who are incautious (2 Co 2:11); he can blind the minds of people, and prevent them grasping the truth (4:4); he can disguise himself as an angel of light, and so trap the unwary (11:14); and he is able to harass the servants of God (12:7).

- ◆ he is quick, and able to take advantage of any opportunity given him by the errors or unbelief of Christians (Ep 4:27), for he has many flaming darts to send against them (6:16).

- ◆ with his mighty armies he contends unceasingly against the church, so that Paul earnestly warns that our conflict is not with

- ◆ "flesh and blood, but against the principalities, against the powers, against the world rulers of this present darkness, against the spiritual hosts of wickedness in the heavenly places" (6:12).

- ◆ to stand safely against the wiles of this cunning and strong foe, we need nothing less than "the whole armour of God" (vs. 11).

♦ again and again he is able to hinder the church in its performance of the will of God (1 Th 2:18), and by his power of temptation he can sometimes frustrate the best labours of God's servants (3:5).

♦ by deceit and demonic doctrines he has caused many to depart from the faith (1 Ti 4:1); he has snared them and made them captives to his will (2 Ti 2:26).

♦ only those who are continually vigilant can be sure of escaping the evil influence of this pitiless adversary, who is ever going about like a roaring lion seeking someone to devour (1 Pe 5:8).

♦ he is still a king, his throne is still intact, he dwells among the cities of men, and he afflicts the church (Re 2:13); his army is like a horde of fierce locusts, and they have power on the earth (9:3). The revelator describes the host of evil:

♦ Like horses arrayed for battle; on their heads were what looked like crowns of gold; their faces were like human faces ... their teeth like lion's teeth; they had scales like breastplates, and the noise of their wings was like the noise of many chariots with horses rushing into battle. They have tails like scorpions, and stings ... They have as king over them the angel of the bottomless pit; his name in Hebrew is Abaddon, and in Greek he is called Apollyon (vs. 7-11).

♦ godless imperialism and corrupt religion are described under the figure of a "beast" - but the beast gains its power and authority from that hideous dragon, the devil (13:1-4). Because of this satanic strength the "beast" has "authority over every tribe and people and tongue and nation" (vs.7); it oppresses the human race, furiously attacks the church, and is seemingly invincible and everywhere triumphant (vs. 11-18).

But the most arresting statement of all, is this -

He was allowed to make war on the saints and to
conquer them (Re 13:7).

Here indeed is the "mystery of iniquity" (2 Th 2:7) - not only that God should have given the devil power to wage war against the saints, but that he also has power "to conquer them".

How can this be? Does God not love his people? Does he not care that they perish? What has happened to the victory of Christ?

IV. WHY DOES GOD ALLOW THIS?

Even devout Christians find their faith troubled when they realise the world is as far away from conversion to Christ as it was two thousand years ago. The kingdom of darkness seems to be waxing ever more mighty. The church in many places is in full retreat. If our doctrines are true, if God does exist, if he is truly Almighty, if Christ has delivered a death blow to the devil, why is the church so feeble and the world so strong? Why is there still so much terrible suffering - wars, famines, bloodshed, violence, hunger, poverty - an unending squalor of pain and haunting misery?

It is easy to sympathise with the masses of humanity who are "scorched by the fierce heat and curse the name of God ... for their pain and sores" (Re 16:9,11,21). Scripture does not fully resolve this mystery, but it does offer two general explanations -

A. THE WORLD IS UNDER THE SWAY OF SATAN

The world of this 20th century is just as much dominated by the powers of evil as the world of the 1st century. Satan is still the prince and ruler of this world. The "Beast" still has authority over every tribe, people, tongue, and nation. The time has not yet come for the destroyer to be himself utterly destroyed. Satan's continued freedom of action, the continued flourishing of evil, the weakened state of the church in many parts of the earth - none of these things mean that God has lost control, nor that the gospel is not true.

On the contrary, the gospel itself teaches that such things must be. As I have shown earlier, the righteous purpose of God prevents him for the present from acting against the kingdom of darkness. God is not defeated, nor are his purposes hindered. By his own decree the world goes on its accustomed way.

But that glorious and ineluctable day will eventually come when all the servants of unrighteousness, whether man or devil, will be suddenly called to face the wrath of God and to be cast down in judgment. Then we shall join the hosts of heaven in the glad shout-

The kingdom of the world has become the kingdom of our Lord and of his Christ, and he shall reign for ever and ever ... We give thanks to thee, Lord God Almighty ... that thou hast taken thy great power and begun to reign. The nations raged, but thy wrath came, and the time for the dead to be judged, for rewarding thy servants ... and for destroying the destroyers of the earth ... Now the salvation and the power and the kingdom of our God and the authority of his Christ have come, for the accuser of our brethren has been thrown down! (Re 11:17-18; 12:12:10).

That day is not yet. But it will be -.

B. A TIME OF TESTING FOR THE SAINTS

We now understand that the troubles afflicting the world are allowed by God to continue, because the day of the Lord's vengeance against Satan has not yet come. But what about the church? Why has God allowed Satan power to "make war on the saints and to conquer them?" Perhaps the answer is given most succinctly in Re 13:10 -

Here is a call for the endurance and faith of the saints.

In the fiery crucible of temptation and affliction, faith is proved genuine and Christ is shown sufficient -

> *Rejoice in this! For a little while you may have to suffer various trials; but this is so that the genuineness of your faith, more precious than gold,*

which though perishable is tested by fire, may redound to praise and glory and honour at the revelation of Jesus Christ" (1 Pe 1:6-7).

Temptation provides an opportunity for us to share in the glory of Christ. By his grace we overcome a foe mightily superior to us in strength and intelligence. Then to us who overcome in Christ, is given this assurance: having shared his victory we shall also share his magnificent inheritance - see Re 2:7,11,17,26- 28; 3:5,12,21; 21:7. To the remainder comes this warning -

But as for the cowardly, the faithless, the polluted, as for murderers, fornicators, sorcerers, idolaters, and all liars, their lot shall be in the lake that burns with fire and brimstone, which is the second death (vs.8).

"In the struggle against Satan there is neither neutrality (Lu 11:23) nor secret treaty-making (Mt 6:24; 1 Co 10:21). Constant watchfulness (1 Pe 5:8), constant preparedness (Ep 6:10) is required, and above all uncompromising sureness of victory! Satan has in fact power only over those who `give him opportunity' (Ep 4:27), who allow themselves to be led astray by the threefold lust (1 Jn 2:16), and thereby open the doors of their thinking, willing, and acting to him. But he who belongs to the body of Christ is withdrawn from the power of Satan: the Lord, the God of peace, will soon crush Satan under his feet (Ro 16:20) and guard that man from `the evil one' (2 Th 3:3; Mt 6:13)."[41]

---

[41]   Bauer, op. cit. pg. 812. Emphasis mine.

CHAPTER FOUR

ABOUT DEMONS

If you are wearing a necklace, or some other pretty piece of jewellery, particularly around your throat or on your head, then you are unknowingly perpetuating a superstition that goes back into the mists of antiquity. Head jewellery was worn by the people of the ancient world as a charm against sickness. It was thought that all disease came from demons that entered the body through the apertures of the head - the mouth, ears, and nose. By using proper spells and charmed jewellery, people believed they would gain protection from these demon invaders. Modern earrings, necklaces, pendants, head-bands, amulets, and the like, are direct descendants of those early talismans.

This union of jewellery with demons is described in a quaint passage from a 3rd century writing, which contains a fictitious sermon by Peter. The apostle tells how demons had intercourse with women, and then, desiring to

> "please their mistresses, instead of themselves, they
> showed the bowels of the earth; I mean, the choice
> metals, gold, brass, silver, iron, and the like, with all
> the most precious stones. And along with these
> charmed stones, they delivered the arts of ... melting
> gold and silver, and the like, and the various dyeing
> of garments. And all things, in short, which are for

> the adornment and delight of women, are the
> discoveries of these demons ... [42]

Our primitive forefathers firmly believed that hosts of evil spirits, some beneficent, some malignant, crowded the air around them. By sacrifices, incantations, religious rituals, and the like, they sought to strengthen the friendship of the benign spirits, and to nullify (or even befriend) those that were malign. People placed firm reliance on various charms and spells, on philtres and divinations, and great care was taken to use exactly the right formula in each case.

The OT is happily free of such hoary mumbo-jumbo. Nevertheless, the demonology of the OT is more complex than is commonly thought. Various kinds of demons are named, and there is a clear belief that without divine protection life would indeed be a fearful thing, haunted and vexed by many evil powers. The demonology of the NT is plainer than that of the OT; yet there also the issues are more enigmatic than may at first appear. For example:

- ♦ no clear link is established between demons and fallen angels, and it remains uncertain if they are the same beings;

- ♦ the prominent place held by demons in the gospels is drastically reduced in the remainder of the NT;

- ♦ in the original Greek, Satan is nowhere called a demon, and no demon is ever called a devil;

- ♦ "principalities and powers" are referred to, but it is often not clear whether the reference is to good or evil beings, nor is there any clear identification of these beings with either good or evil angels, or with demons;

---

[42]   The article on Principalities and Powers" in Bauer (op. cit.) discusses in some depth the uncertainty of these matters and the impossibility of resolving them only from the NT data.

♦ no indication is given of the origin of these principalities, nor of the origin of angels, nor of demons, nor of Satan; and so on.

♦ we are told nothing about the nature of demon possession; nor how demons attack humans, how they release their victims, what happens when people are attacked or loosed.

♦ we cannot tell how many demons there are, nor how extensive is their presence in human society, nor whether they can escape the bounds of this planet.

It is true that Christians do commonly identify demons with fallen angels (as I have done above), and they usually identify the "principalities and powers" with both good and evil angels; but the NT itself does not clearly establish these links.[43] In this chapter, I want to look at the OT data; then glance at the traditions the Jews added to the OT; and then examine more fully the things taught in the NT. Many questions will be answered, but many must remain obscure.

I. DEMONS IN THE OT

A. VARIOUS KINDS OF DEMONS

The Hebrew word for "demon" occurs with certainty only twice in the OT - "They sacrificed to demons which were no gods, to gods they had never known" ... "They sacrificed their sons and daughters to demons" (De 32:17; Ps 106:37). There is perhaps a third reference in Le 17:7, "They must no longer offer any of their

---

[43] Some commentators maintain that the Hebrew text should be emended to read "demons" (*shedhim*) also in the following places: Ge 14:3,8,10; Jb 5:23.

sacrifices to the goat-idols (or demons) to whom they prostitute themselves."[44]

Both of those references indicate that behind the practice of idolatry there did lie a spiritual reality. Diabolical forces were at work to entice the people, and to persuade them by occult powers to believe that the gods they served were not just graven images, but real gods. This offers some explanation for the continual tendency of the people to stray from the Lord and to attach themselves to Canaanite deities. The gods of the heathen often seemed more immediately and visibly powerful than did the true God.

The word translated "demon" is *shedh*, which was a Chaldean/Assyrian word adopted into the Hebrew tongue. The original sense of *shedh* was simply that of a spiritual being, one with divine powers, whether good or evil. Among early peoples there was no clear distinction between good or evil spirits. Spirits that were usually benevolent might have their times of venom; while malicious spirits could be persuaded to act benevolently. However, when the Israelites took *shedh* into their tongue they gave it a wholly sinister meaning, for they used it only to describe a particular group of vicious and hostile demons. In the main, these demons were identical with Canaanite field or desert spirits. They were the evil genius behind pagan idolatry.

Generally, the Hebrews had little fear of demons, but they placed these *shedhim* in a special category of spirits, which were a source of many dreads among the people. The origin of the *shedhim* was usually thought to be unknown. Sometimes the people linked them with fallen angels, sometimes with the offspring of a hideous union between corrupt angels and human mothers. And there were other popular superstitions.

---

[44]   Ante-Nicene Fathers, Vol 8.; "*The Clementine Homilies*," (8.14); pg 273.

The OT acknowledges the existence of the *shedhim*, but gives no clue as to their origin.

1. "Satyrs"

Because the main group of field demons were supposed to resemble hairy he-goats (Hebrew, *sah-geer*), they were called "satyrs" - Le 17:7; 2 Ch 11:15; Is 13:21; 34:14. The satyrs were often worshipped by Israel, and since they were field-demons, sacrifices were usually offered to them in some open place. Jeroboam even appointed priests to officiate at their worship. One of these satyrs became prominent enough in the fears of the people to receive a personal name (Azazel) and to occupy a special place in the rituals ordained by Moses (Le 16:8 ff.) - but I will discuss Azazel more fully below.

Satyrs, people whispered, haunted the open fields, and particularly desert places (cp. Lu 8:29) At certain times you could hear their eerie cries and yells. And woe to the unlucky person who heard that dread sound! This is the probable origin of the expression "the howling waste" (De 32:10; and cp. Is 13:21) -

> To be imprisoned in the viewless winds,
> And blown with restless violence round about
> The pendant world; or to be worse than worst
> Of those that lawless and uncertain thoughts
> Imagine howling: 'tis too horrible!
> - Shakespeare, "Measure For Measure" (III.i.114)

2. "Evil Spirits"

Another class of demon was thought to be more closely involved with human society, directly attacking and troubling men and women. So we read of "evil spirits" (Jg. 9:23; 1 Sa. 16:14; 18:10; 19:9); and of "lying spirits" (1 Kg. 22:22- 23); and of the devil provoking Israel to sin, and thus bringing a plague upon the people (1 Ch. 21:1; and cf. also Job 1:12 ff.). The reference in Is. 19:14 to a "spirit of confusion" may also have demonic overtones, along with such references as Jg 9:23 (the spirit of discord); 1 Kg 22:19-

23 (the spirit of lies); Is 19:14 (the spirit of giddiness); and 29:10 (the spirit of lethargy).

These spirits are distinct from the field demons. They are more closely connected with the true spiritual realm; they are not restricted to a particular locality; they are able to attack people in their own homes, and at any time; but they can do so only by permission of the Lord and only when the person attacked has given some cause to be so afflicted.

3. "Lilith" - The Night Hag, and Others

"There shall the night hag alight, and find for herself a resting place" (Is 34:14).

The "night hag" was originally a Mesopotamian female demon called Lilith, an alluring wraith who tempted men through erotic dreams. But over the centuries her appearance and her role changed. By the time she reached Palestine and became part of Jewish demonology, she had been transformed into an ugly night demon. She spread fear by prowling among ruins, lurking in desolate places, and seeking to steal children when she found them alone, lost, or straying from their homes. Parents used the terror of Lilith to stop their children from wandering away. The Talmud describes her as Adam's first wife (given to him before Eve); but because she refused to submit to him she was banished to the upper air, from which she returns at night to haunt her victims.

According to Delitzsch, "Lilith, the creature of the night, was a female demon of the popular mythology; according to the legends, it was a malicious fairy that was especially hurtful to children, like some of the fairies of our own fairy tales."[45]

A very old Canaanite inscription has been found, containing a spell against the wiles of this hag of the night -

---

[45]   Op. cit. Commentary on Isaiah, in loc.

> "An incantation for the female flying demon. To the
> female demon that flies in the dark chamber, say:
> Pass by, time and again, O Lilith!"[46]

Lilith was often thought of as a vampire demon who sucked the blood of sleeping victims. Because of this, some commentators see another reference to her in Pr 30:15, which could be translated, "The female blood-sucker has two daughters; `Give, give', they cry ... "

Similarly, "pestilence" and "the destroyer", mentioned in Ps 91:6, may be personalised names for particular demons; perhaps they should have initial capitals. Some commentators call "the destroyer" mentioned in Ex 12:23 a demon servant of the Lord, who could be warded off only by a blood-talisman. Others, however, deny there is any allusion to demons in those verses.

Did Isaiah believe in the existence of Lilith? Did he approve the popular myths about this Chaldean demon? Does scripture endorse the superstitious fears of ancient Israel and her neighbours? It seems more probable that Isaiah used Lilith simply as a literary device. It is unlikely he accepted the reality of this evil crone. He spoke about her merely to highlight the total ruin that was to come upon Edom (vs. 8-9, ff.)

However, just the fact that Isaiah mentions Lilith shows that the myths about her were familiar to his original readers. No doubt many of them believed in her evil powers, and were haunted by a dread of desolate places, or of being alone in a ruined building at night. Also, behind the superstition there certainly stood the reality of true demons who were an actual menace to human health and happiness.

---

[46]   The Ancient Near East, Vol. II; ed. J. B. Pritchard; Princeton University Press, 1975; pg 220.

4. "Rahab"

See Jb 9:13; 26:12; Ps 87:4; 89:10; Is 30:7; 51:9-10.

In popular mythology, Rahab was a female demon who held primordial power over the forces of nature, particularly over the oceans. Most commentators equate Rahab with Tiamut, a Babylonian female monster whom the myths associated with the primeval chaos. God is pictured as entering into conflict with Rahab (that is, Chaos) and overcoming her by a mighty display of divine strength. The creative triumph of Yahweh over Rahab is absolute. The monsters of disorder, Leviathan and the Abyss, flee in terror from the creative fiat of the Lord God.

The prophets turned the myths into poetic illustrations of how Yahweh moved upon the dark and troubled waters of the great deep, and out of Chaos created order and beauty (Ge 1:1-2).

Because Israel's escape from Egypt was made possible by dividing the waters of the Red Sea (part of Rahab's domain), the exodus is described under the symbolism of God smiting Rahab; and from this link with the exodus, the title Rahab was extended to include Egypt. You will need to decide from the context the sense the word has in each example.

While many of the people may have believed that Rahab was a real demon, it is not likely the biblical writers did so. Nonetheless, the references to her do show a belief that powerful spiritual forces are at work in the world. Demonic influence may sometimes lie behind the violence of nature. In that sense, the references to Rahab do reflect spiritual reality.

5. "Baalzebub"

Baalzebub (also called Beelzebub, or Beelzebul) was a Philistine demon god. He was the chief god of Ekron; but he had a sufficient reputation beyond that city to lead Ahaziah to seek his help (see 2 Kg 1:2; Mt 12:24; Mk 3:22; Lu 11:15).

"Baalzebub" probably means "Lord of the Flies". Why he was given such an unusual name is unknown. Perhaps the people thought of their god as moving swiftly like the fly; or like flies, which are found everywhere and have all-round vision, they believed Baalzebub was ubiquitous and all-seeing. The NT changes his name to Beelzebul, which may also mean Lord of the Flies. But some commentators prefer to read it "Lord of the Dung-heap", in which case there is no link between Beelzebul and the OT demon-god.

The NT links Beelzebul with Satan, and speaks of him as the prince of demons; but it remains uncertain if Satan and Beelzebul are the same being. Beelzebul may simply be the chief of all the demons, perhaps second only to the devil himself. If Beelzebul and Baalzebub are identical, he has the distinction (with the possible exception of Abaddon) of being the only demon specifically mentioned in the OT whose real existence the NT confirms.

6. "Abaddon"

See Jb 26:56; 28:22; 31:12; Ps 88:121; Pr 15:11; 27:20; Re 9:11. The name means "The Destroyer". It was originally applied to Sheol, because that is where the dead were destroyed. But when the concept of life beyond the grave became more developed, Abaddon was gradually restricted to the very lowest regions of Sheol. Soon it described only the place of special torment and punishment of the wicked.

Still later in Jewish thought Abaddon was personified. It became the name of the demon prince of the nethermost parts of Gehenna, the deepest deeps of hell. It is in this sense that John described him-

> *They have as king over them the angel of the bottomless pit; his name in Hebrew is Abaddon, and in Greek he is called Apollyon (Re 9:11).*

If the presence of this demon prince can be seen in the OT references to Abaddon, then (as I have said) he shares with Baalzebub the distinction of being one of the only two demons whose existence both testaments acknowledge.

The "bottomless pit" (or "abyss") had several different meanings in Bible days. It could describe the vast and terrible dwelling place of all the evil spirits; but it might also mean the place of confinement and punishment of those same spirits (cp. Lu 8:31). Paul used "abyss" in a reference to the drama of Jesus' death and burial (Ro 10:7); and it will be the place of Satan's final imprisonment (Re 20:1-3).

The picture conveyed is that the abyss is the usual habitation of the devil and his angels. But located at its very centre is the dread lake of fire reserved for their eventual endless torment. Christ's descent into the abyss and his subsequent resurrection and ascension, are marks of his conquest of Satan. The kingdom of darkness must call him Lord. The inability of the devil and his angels finally to escape the abyss is a guarantee of their future punishment in the lake of fire.

7. "Azazel"

See Le 16:8, 10, 26. "Azazel" was a desert-spirit. The references to him reflect the prevalent ancient belief that the desert was in a peculiar sense the dwelling place of many demons. Azazel was thought to be the leader of the evil spirits of the wilderness. The later Jews also thought of him as one of the chief leaders of the angels who fell with Satan and were cast out of heaven.

Notice in the references above that "Azazel" is not the name of the scapegoat, as is commonly thought, for that animal was "sent away into the wilderness to Azazel". Notice that the scapegoat was not a sacrifice offered to a demon; rather, it symbolised the transfer of sin from the realm of living men to the already hopelessly corrupt realm of Satan -

"Azazel's function was to receive the second of the two goats that were used in the atonement service (Le 16:7,8). The first, as determined by lot, was offered to Yahweh as a sin offering (vs. 9; cp. vs. 5). The second, or (es)scape-goat, however is not called a sin offering, nor was it killed: God's people are not to sacrifice to demons (De 32:17). Its significance lies rather in the fact that the sins of the people were confessed over it (vs. 21) and that it was sent away, allowed to escape alive, into the wilderness for Azazel. In this way the scapegoat made atonement for the people (vs. 10). The two-fold truth that is symbolised is this: the release of Israel from the grip of sin as caused by Satan, and the subsequent taking back of these sins to their demonic author.

"The fulfilment of this Mosaic type occurred when Christ took upon himself the sins of the redeemed, thereby suffering separation from God the Father (Mt 27:46), but `through death bringing to nought him that had the power of death, that is the devil' (He 2:15,16) ... Our Lord's penal sufferings were clearly a ransom to God, and not to Satan; but still, `to this end was the Son of God manifested, that he might destroy the works of the devil' (1 Jn. 3:8)."[47]

8. "Leviathan"

See Jb 3:8; 7:12; 40:25; Ps 74:14; 104:26; Is 27:1; 51:9; Am 9:3. Like Rahab, Leviathan in popular mythology was a powerful god who presided over the primeval chaos. People saw him as an immense twisting sea-serpent, and sometimes as a huge water-dragon. His thrashings caused terrible storms and threatened to tear the world apart. But by an irresistible command God subdued him, and order prevailed over disorder. Job 3:8 refers to a primitive fear that a skilful curse against the natural order might again arouse Leviathan to furious action and bring ruin upon the people.

Did the prophets share that fear? Probably not. While rejecting the mythology, they used the old superstitions to give poetical colour to their predictions of Yahweh's conquest of all dark forces. But their more naive readers were sure that this demon, and others in the ancient hellish pantheon, were real and active. The same could be said about Isaiah's description of -

---

[47]   J. Barton-Payne, op. cit. pg. 292,293.

9. "The Flying Serpent"

See Is 14:29; 30:6. This demon is also called the Saraph-Serpent, or the Basilisk. He is possibly referred to also in Ps 90:13, which in the Vulgate reads, "Thou shalt tread upon the asp and the basilisk."

The ancients held the basilisk in great terror. Death seized anyone touched by its awful stench, or upon whom its breath or even look should fall. Like a dragon, it breathed fire, and delighted to drive men crazy with thirst in desert places. The only way to kill it, was to hold a mirror before its face. The demon, beholding its own ugliness, and peering into the horror of its own eyes, would be instantly slain.

The power of the basilisk to capture its victims by a mere glance, became a favourite theme of poets and preachers. They saw in it an analogy of a wily woman, who by a single look fascinates and slays her hapless lover -

> Many may escape from rope and gun;
> Nay, some have outlived the doctor's pill:
> Who takes a woman must be undone,
> That basilisk is sure to kill!
> - John Gay (1688-1732), "The Beggar's Opera," I.viii.26.

Scripture knows nothing about that analogy, of course; but many a medieval teacher saw in the basilisk a salutary warning against fleshy indulgence! They also saw a picture of Christ's victory over the devil. This fiery serpent might be a king (Greek, *basileus*), but he would be surely trodden underfoot by the King of kings!

B. ISRAEL AND HER NEIGHBOURS

Two general observations can be made about OT demonology:

- ♦ it does reflect a clear belief in the kingdom of darkness, along with a firm recognition that divine protection is both necessary and available.

- ♦ nevertheless, the people of Israel usually had a low awareness of Satan and/or demons. Think how sparse the references are, across a period of some 2000 years of Hebrew history.

That is why the Sadducees, in the time of Christ, denied the existence of angels and the resurrection. Not because they did not believe the scriptures, but because they refused to accept anything not clearly taught in the writings of Moses. By contrast, the Pharisees gave an authority to their own oral traditions almost equal to that of the Bible.

Here is something for you to ponder. The people of Israel were able for twenty centuries to serve God quite well, despite an almost negligible awareness of the devil. Contrast that with some modern charismatics, who seem to think it necessary to be constantly chasing after demons even to survive, let alone flourish!

Israel's scant attention during most of its history to the demonic world is astonishing when it is compared with culture of all her neighbours. Without exception, superstition saturated those other nations. They lived in a world haunted by myriads of evil spirits -

"The ordinary man saw himself surrounded by forces which to him were gods or devils. There was a raging demon who manifested himself in the sand-storm sweeping in from the desert, and the man who opposed this demon was likely to be smitten with painful sinusitis. Fire was a god. The river was a god, and at the Ordeal, in which an accused person had to jump into the water, would seize the wicked man who perjured himself. The shimmering light that appeared upon the mountains just before sunrise was the glow from the haloes of the scorpion-men who guarded the sun at his ascent. A host of demons stood always ready to seize a man or woman in particular circumstances, as, in lonely places, when eating or drinking, in sleep, and particularly in childbirth. The gods themselves were not exempt from the attacks of demons, and the eclipse of the moon was considered a case of the Moon-god. Sin having been temporarily vanquished by these beings ... "[48]

"The ritual with which (talismans were) set up for the protection of a house have been largely recovered. It began with an enumeration of possible causes of the misfortune of the house:

> `Whether it be an evil ghost or an evil spook or an evil ghoul or an evil god or an evil Croucher or a Lamashtu or a Labasu or the Seizer or Lilu, Lilith, or a handmaid of Lilu, or the Hand-of-a-god or the Hand-of-a-goddess, or Epidemic, ... or Plague-demon or the Bad-luck demon ... or Death or Heat or Fever or the Killer ... whatever there may be ... which does harm to a man, in a man's house ... '

"Instructions were then given for the preparation of the figures of wood and clay to protect the house:

> `You shall sprinkle holy water; set up a cult- stand; offer lambs for sacrifice and bring the hams, lard, and roast meat; scatter dates and fine meal; set out a confection of honey and butter; set up a censer with juniper-wood; pour out a wine libation; do obeisance, purify the censer, torch, holy-water vessel and tamarisk wood, and speak thus ... ' (then follow the words of the incantation).[49]

Israel's contemporaries all had similar superstitions. They lived under constant threat of demonic attack. They threaded their lives with countless ceremonies to ward off malevolent spirits, to placate malicious gods, to turn spiteful jinns into friendly ones, and so on.

---

[48]   The Greatness That Was Babylon, by H. W. F. Saggs; Sidgwick & Jackson, London, 1969; pg. 302.

[49]   Ibid. pg. 314.

The singular lack of such things in the OT, unlike all other sacred writings of those times, is a remarkable sign of its inspiration and of how astonishingly different Israel was among the nations of the ancient world.

C. TRADITIONAL DEVELOPMENTS

The references I have so far given nearly exhaust the OT data on demons. As you can see, it is sparse and indeterminate. There is evidence that Israelite beliefs about demons were influenced by the demonologies of the surrounding nations; yet it is also clear that the Hebrews were generally not fearful of demons, and they rejected most of the wilder superstitions and dreads of their neighbours.

Even when demons are specifically named, it is probable that the Hebrews (or the more godly among them) were simply using popular terminology without intending to endorse all that was vulgarly believed about those demons.

The OT leaves many questions about demons unanswered. It offers no clue about their origin or destiny. It gives no indication if they are fallen angels, or some other form of being. It tends as much as possible to ignore them. When it does mention them, no doubt remains that they are wholly subservient to the Lord God and that they have no power to harm the righteous. In the main, the OT treatment of demons, in remarkable contrast to contemporary Egyptian, Mesopotamian, and Canaanite documents, is sober, restrained, dignified, and set within a framework of strict monotheism.

But the captivity in Babylon and the Persian conquest introduced the Jews to a much more complex and fearsome demonology, and this is reflected in later Jewish literature. By the time of Christ the Jews had moved far away from the restraint of their fathers. Like their neighbours, they now had names for scores of different demons, and they had accumulated a great mass of traditions, myths, and legends. I have gathered a few of these together -

1. The Apocrypha

The most well known example occurs in the apocryphal story of Tobit (3:8,ff), which describes the murders committed by "Asmodeus, that worst of demons." Asmodeus was a Persian spirit, "the prince of lust", whom the Jews took into their own demonology, although in a different character.

Even more quaint than the skill of Asmodeus in destroying Sarah's happiness by killing her seven bridegrooms "one after another before ever they had slept with her as man with wife", was the charm Raphael prescribed to rid her of the demon. The angel was confident that smoke from a burning fish's heart and liver would suffice to drive away any demon or evil spirit, "leaving no trace" of its former presence (6:7-8, 17-18).

Tobias heeded this angelic wisdom, "went to his bag, took the fish's heart and liver out of it and put some on the burning incense. The reek of the fish distressed the demon, who fled thought the air to Egypt. Raphael pursued him there, and bound and shackled him at once" (8:1-3).

Other non-canonical Jewish literature abounds with references to demons of many kinds who performed all kinds of prodigies, and who required various charms and spells to drive them away. Some of these demons were thought to have sprung from a foul union between women and fallen angels - an idea based on a particular interpretation of Ge. 6:1-4. The "mighty men" born to these women were in their turn thought to have become demons when they died. These demons were all said to be malevolent to a greater or lesser degree, and to cause great mischief among men.

Gradually, most of the grievous hurts that afflict mankind were attributed to a demon of one sort or another.

One Jewish tradition supposed that God created demons on Friday - hence the popular superstition, still current, that this day is one of ill omen. Another tradition thought that demons were the ghosts of wicked men, while the spirits of good men, it was said, became angels. Another tradition claimed that demons were souls created by God, but before he had time to fashion their bodies the Sabbath dawned, and God had to leave them unfinished - thus they were neither men nor angels.

It was usually thought that demons could become visible or invisible at will, and that they could assume any shape - except they preferred a human form. However, one could always recognise them: their feet were webbed, or shaped like a fowl's, and they had no shadow.

Other traditions said that demons preferred waterless places (cp. Lu 11:24), for water was the means of cleansing, particularly if ritually used. The night hours were especially haunted by demon activity. For this reason, since the night belonged to evil spirits, and since water was an affront to them, drinking water at night was thought to be an invitation to demon attack.

Another popular notion was that demons resembled people in having a necessity to eat and drink, and in being able to propagate their own kind. But others insisted that they were wholly spirits, having no physical properties, and no procreative powers. Many Jews believed that while demons could understand all languages, the angels could understand only Hebrew, the "holy tongue" - hence all races were plagued by demons, but the Hebrews alone could call on the angels for help.

However, not all the Hebrews believed such superstitions. People who revered the scriptures and had a vital relationship with God scorned pagan myths. Note that while some of the Apocrypha contain references to the popular and foolish demonology (e.g. Tobit), the more serious works, such as Wisdom and

Ecclesiasticus, scarcely mention demons at all. Indeed, their best spiritual concepts are as noble as those found in the canonical writings. Baruch in fact warned the people that they had suffered captivity in Babylon for the very fault of angering God by trying to placate spurious demons, and he urged them to cling to the Lord alone (Bar 4:7).

It is also worth noting that some of these ancient superstitions are still prevalent among the ignorant and the gullible, and the same kind of curiosity about the preternatural world that led our forefathers to such wild speculation is not lacking from some parts of the modern church. I have read some so-called Christian books on demon possession and exorcism which, for sheer inanity and credulity, equal anything the ancients ever produced. Their doctrines are closer to the spirit of pagan Babylon than they are to the scriptures.

II. DEMONS AND THE EARLY CHURCH

The demonology of the NT is much more obvious than that of the OT, but there are several puzzling aspects to it. Some of these I have mentioned already, but we need to examine them more fully -

A. CONTRAST AND SILENCE

What is your picture of Satan? Do you see him as a powerful monarch, ruling over a vast and complex kingdom, with hierarchies of fallen angels and demons? You should realise there is little of that scene in the OT; it appears without explanation in the gospels. Suddenly, there he is. A being of awesome power. Warring continually against the servants of God, and even against God himself.

At best the OT contains only allusions to such a warfare in the heavenlies (cp. Jb 21:22; 25:2; and other references to the angels as the "armies" of God). There is nothing in the OT that approaches the NT picture of the kingdom of darkness, with its "principalities and powers", its law of unrelenting hate, its death struggle against righteousness, its final overthrow in a cataclysmic act of divine judgment.

How strange the vivid gospel etching of Satan appears when it is set alongside the shadowy image of the OT. The devil is almost absent from the history and prophecies of Israel. He may (as we have seen) be the Serpent who tempted Adam and Eve; and he appears in the story of Job, with a surprising freedom of access to the throne of God (1:6; 2:1); and there are a couple of other OT references. But usually the story of Israel unfolds without paying any attention to the devil. It has to be significant that for generations God-fearing people were able to live successfully without ever thinking about Satan. That is something for you to ponder!

There are other mysteries -

1. Things We Don't Know

a. Scripture offers no explanation for the remarkably well-developed concept of demon possession that is so prominent in the gospels, but is almost wholly lacking from the OT. There is no exact OT parallel for the kind of demon possession described so often in the NT (particularly in the gospels and Acts). The OT spans a history of at least 4000 years, yet there is not one clear case described in the whole period of either demon possession or of exorcism (the closest examples are 1 Sa 16:14-16,23; 18:10; 19:9).

What is true of the contrast between the NT and the OT, is also true to a lesser extent between the gospels and the remainder of the NT. The profusion of references to demons in the gospels is much lessened in Acts, and disappears almost entirely from the letters. This has led some commentators to suppose that the phenomenon of demon possession was especially associated with the ministry of Jesus - as though hell stirred itself to a frenzy of opposition against the Christ during those three crucial years.

But there is a problem with that view: neither the gospels, nor the people described in them, appear to have expressed any surprise at the incidence of demon possession then occurring in Palestine. The real cause of amazement was the authority of Jesus over the demons. But everybody seems to have accepted as normal the presence of the demons themselves, and of their victims.

b. Despite what might be thought a reasonable expectation, scripture gives no explanation of the origin of Satan, nor of the demons he is presumed to have under his control. The NT is as silent on these matters as is the OT. It may, for example, be fair to infer (as I have done above) that the fallen angels described in Jude and 2 Peter are the source of demons and evil spirits, but the NT itself does not clearly make that identification. There are actually some objections to the idea: the fallen angels, we are told, are incarcerated in Tartarus, while demons obviously have a high degree of freedom.

If fallen angels and demons are not identical, then we have no information at all on the origin of demons. It is interesting to note that the early church for a long time maintained a clear distinction between demons and fallen angels. The fusion of the identity of these two was a later innovation in Christian thought.

c. The nature of demon possession itself; the limits of such possession; who can be possessed; how possession takes place; whether Christians can be possessed; how to recognise possession in contrast with other kinds of affliction, both natural and preternatural - the NT explains none of this. The writers apparently assumed that such things were already known to their readers; or perhaps they were not sure about the answers themselves.

d. Demon possession is nowhere treated as a doctrine in the Bible. It happens only as an event, without any attempt to explain the origin or the underlying nature of the event. No NT writing contains any instruction about exorcism.

That demons do attack people is accepted (especially in the gospels, but to a much lesser degree elsewhere) as a fact of human life. But the apostles apparently gave little time to thinking about it. One evangelist, John, ignored it altogether. There is not a single reference to exorcism in his gospel. Nor is there any mention of casting out demons in any NT letters.

This sparsity of references to the devil and demons in many of the most important NT documents surely says something about the minor place that such ideas had in the thinking of the apostles. Apart from recording what they had observed, particularly in the ministry of Jesus, and occasionally in Acts, they had virtually nothing to say about the subject. We are left to wonder why. It may not be unfair to point out that their prudence and restraint stands in sharp contrast to the intemperate and irresponsible speculation indulged in by some modern authors.

But I have to admit that they do have companions going far back into history. There is something about this subject that compels people to want to know more than God has been pleased to reveal. So from early times Jewish and Christian leaders have theorised on the origin and nature of demons. Here are some of the commoner notions -

2. Common Speculations

a. Demons are the spirits of human beings whom God had not finished when the Sabbath began; therefore he had to leave them unclothed with bodies. From this arose the superstition that Friday is unlucky.

b. They are the spirits of the wicked, condemned to roam the earth after their bodies had perished in the grave. This was the belief of a group of philosophers called the Platonists. Augustine draws attention to it (City Of God, Bk. IX, ch. 11). He considered it dangerous nonsense.

c. They are the spirits of the "giants" who died after they had been born from an unnatural union between certain angels and women (cp. Ge 6:1-4). The Jews were fond of this view, and it was popular in the early church.

d. The Clementine Homilies contain a peculiar theory that demons came into existence when -

> "the angels who dwell in the lowest region, being grieved at the ingratitude of men to God, asked that they might come into the life of men, that, really becoming men, by more intercourse they might convict those who had acted ungratefully towards (God) and might subject everyone to adequate punishment... (Unhappily, despite their good intentions, when these angels did assume human form and became) in all respects men, they also partook of human lust, and being brought under its subjection they fell into co-habitation with women, and being involved with them, and sunk in defilement and altogether emptied of their first power, were unable to turn back to the first purity of their proper nature ... "[50]

♦ So, being unable to return to their heavenly form and habitation, they became demons! The theory seems to be an attempt to escape the insuperable difficulty of imagining how angels, who are spirit, can have sexual relations with women, who are flesh.

e. They are the spirits of people who after death were elevated to a higher plane of existence; but instead of choosing to advance closer to heaven, they yearned still for the pleasures of the earth, and so became hateful and rebellious.

f. They are the product of an attempt by certain angels to unite themselves with human nature in order to steal the special God-image built into men and women.

---

[50] Op. cit. Homily 8, ch. 12,13.

g. They are fallen angels. This is the prevalent modern view; but as we have seen, there is nothing in scripture to show any link between angels and demons.

h. Here are some more opinions from the Fathers -

ORIGEN (c. 200). "Before the ages minds were all pure, both demons and souls and angels, offering service to God and keeping his commandments. But the devil, who was one of them, since he possessed free-will, desired to resist God, and God drove him away. With him revolted all the other powers. Some sinned deeply, and became demons; others less, and became angels; others still less, and became archangels; and thus each in turn received the reward for his individual sin. But there remained some souls who had not sinned so greatly as to become demons, nor on the other hand so lightly as to become angels. God therefore made the present world, and bound the soul to the body as a punishment."[51]

But another Father argued against the idea that demons are the spirits of wicked men -

TATIAN (c. 150). "The demons who rule over men are not the souls of men, for how should these be capable of such action after death? unless man, who while living was void of understanding and power, should be believed when dead to be endowed with more active power ... It is difficult to conceive that the immortal soul, which is impeded by the members of the body, should become more intelligent when it has migrated from it ... "He

---

[51]   De Principiis, I.8.i; "Ante-Nicene Fathers," Vol. 4.

preferred the teaching that is most common in our time, that demons are fallen angels: That first-begotten one, Satan, through his transgression and ignorance became a demon; and they who imitated him ... are become a host of demons."[52]

AUGUSTINE leaves the interpretation of Ge 6:1-4 unresolved. He doubts that spirit-beings could truly have had intercourse with women, and he is inclined to think that "the sons of God" were at least in some sense human. At least they were not angels, whether fallen or otherwise.[53]

IRENAEUS (c. 150), however, favourably cites the apocryphal book of Enoch, which taught the popular Jewish view that "the sons of God" who took wives from "the daughters of men" were fallen angels.[54] The idea flourished for centuries. It was a common view in Milton's time (Paradise Lost, Bk 1, 323-431). And it has continued down to the present.

Another famous Father thought that demons came from copulation between angels and women -

JUSTIN MARTYR (c. 120). "The angels trans-gressed (God's) appointment, and were captivated by love of women, and begat children who are those that are called demons; and besides, they afterwards subdued the human race to themselves, partly by

---

[52] Ibid. Vol 2; To The Greeks, ch. 16 & ch. 7.

[53] City Of God, Bk. XV, ch. 23.

[54] Against Heresies, ch. 16. "Ante-Nicene Fathers," Vol. 1. The LXX translators held the same view: " ... the angels of God looked upon the daughters of men, saw that they were beautiful, and chose whoever they pleased for wives ... "

magical writings, and partly by fears and the punishments they occasioned, and partly by teaching them to offer sacrifices, and incense, and libations, of which things they stood in need after they were enslaved by lustful passions ..."[55]

But in his debate with Justin, Trypho the Jew strongly objected to the idea that demons were either fallen angels or produced by fallen angels. He called the notion blasphemous. And on this matter there were Christians who would have agreed with the Jew, and Jews who would have agreed with the Christian!

ATHENAGORAS (c. 180) describes fallen angels as copulating with women and producing giants, whose souls after death became demons. He then claimed that the fallen angels now haunt the atmosphere between heaven and earth, while the demons pester the people on earth.[56]

(See also Tertullian, c. 200, for an extended statement on the origin and works of the powers of darkness. Apology, ch. 22, 23.)

i. To round off this section, let us move outside the church and get a pagan opinion on the origin of demons. John Dryden (1631-1700), in his translation of Plutarch's Lives, wrote:

"I will only touch (Plutarch's) belief of spirits ... We have formerly shown that he owned the unity of the Godhead; whom according to his attributes, he calls by several names, as Jupiter from his mighty attributes, Apollo from his wisdom, and so of the rest; but under him he places those beings whom he

---

[55] Ibid. Vol. 1; Apology, Bk. 2, ch. 5.

[56] A Plea For Christians, ch. 24, 25.

styles Genii or Daemons, of a middle nature, between divine and human; for he thinks it absurd that there should be no mean between the two extremes of an immortal and a mortal being; that there cannot be in nature so vast a flaw, without some intermediate kind of life, partaking of them both. As, therefore, we find the intercourse between the soul and body to be made by animal spirits, so between divinity and humanity there is this species of daemons.

"Those who, having first been men, and followed the strict rules of virtue, have purged off the grossness and feculency of their earthly being, are exalted into these Genii; and are from thence either raised higher into an ethereal life, if they still continue virtuous, or tumbled down again into mortal bodies, sinking into flesh after they have lost that purity which constituted their glorious being. And this sort of Genii are those who, as our author (Plutarch) imagines, presided over oracles; spirits which have so much of their terrestrial principles remaining in them as to be subject to passions and inclinations; usually beneficent, sometimes malevolent to mankind, according as they refine themselves, or gather dross, and are declining into mortal bodies ... "[57]

---

[57] Plutarch's Lives, tr. by John Dryden, Modern Library edition, published by Random House, New York; undated; from the Introduction by A. H. Clough, pg. xx, xxi. Plutarch (fl. 100), was a Greek essayist and biographer, who became a pagan priest in his later life. His Lives is a rich source of anecdotal and historical material about the great heroes of the ancient Greek and Roman worlds.

3. *Confident Affirmations*

Turning aside from the speculations of past and present teachers, there are four things we can affirm with confidence about the nature of demons -

a. they are malevolent personal spirits who are at war with God and man; and they are the agents of Satan in destroying human life and happiness.

b. they attack people physically, emotionally, mentally, spiritually, and socially.

c. Christ has gained for every believer absolute victory over all demonic forces.

d. We enter into the victory of Christ in two ways: by personal appropriation of the benefits of the covenant; and by the laying-on of hands in Jesus' name. But by whatever means, God calls you and me to live with full authority over Satan and all his foul minions.

The next chapter will take up this theme of demonic attack upon human life, and how we can turn aside the fiery darts of the wicked one.

But before turning there, let us return for a moment to the theme that opened this chapter, the link between idols and demons -

B. WHAT THE FATHERS THOUGHT

1. Demons And Miracles

Do you remember how the prophets saw the power of demons behind the stone gods the heathen worshipped? The church Fathers, who lived in a hopelessly idolatrous world, infested by a thousand deceitful fables, loudly echoed the same view. Their writings abound with references to their belief that demons were the power behind the gods and goddesses of the pagan temples (cp. 1 Co 10:19-22). Whatever "miracles" these false gods were supposed to have wrought were surely done by the devil. Here is one striking passage from Augustine (354-430), bishop of Hippo, and one of the greatest of the Fathers -

> "When I speak of the miracles of the gods of the gentiles, which history vouches for ... I am talking about the phenomena which are quite evidently the result of the force and power of demons: like the story that the images of the Penates, carried from Troy by Aeneas in his flight, removed themselves from one place to another; the feat of Traquinius in cutting a whetstone with a razor; the serpent from Epidaurus accompanying Aesculapius on his voyage to his Rome; the ship which conveyed the Phrygian Mother, which stuck fast and resisted all the efforts of men and oxen, but was set in motion and drawn along by one mere woman, with her girdle attached to it, a testimony of her chastity; the Vestal Virgin, under suspicion of violating her vows, who put an end to the question by filling a sieve with water from the Tiber without losing any ... "

Augustine was too credulous, although he did no more than share the beliefs of his fellows. I have noticed, for example, that the pagan historian Livy soberly records many prodigies that we would question, if not scorn; but he evidently accepted them as fact. Augustine continues -

> "It seems that the demons can raise the operations of the magicians (our scriptures call them `sorcerers' and `enchanters') to such a pitch of efficiency that Virgil ... wrote these lines about a woman who was a great mistress of that kind of art:
>
> > `She promises with spells to soothe man's mind'
> > If she so will, or to inflict harsh sorrow;
> > To stop the flow of rivers, turn the stars

Back on their course. She will rouse the
spirits
That haunt the night; and you will feel the
earth
Groaning beneath your feet, and from the
mountains
Behold the trees descending to the plain.'

"At this point we shall probably be told that the
pagan gods have performed some miracles ... (But)
the miracles allegedly performed in the pagan
temples are not worthy of comparison with those
performed at the shrines of our martyrs ...
Moreover, the pagan marvels are the work of
demons, in the arrogance of their foul pride which
made them ambitious to be the gods of the
pagans."[58]

Similarly, the Christian apologist Tatian (c. 150) describes
deceptive miracles of healing wrought by demons. But then he
says -

"The demons don't cure, but by their art make men
their captives ... For, just as it is the practice of
some men to capture other persons, and then to
restore them to their friends on payment of a
ransom, so those (demons invade) the bodies of
certain persons ... (and then) command those
persons to come forth into the public, (so that) in
the sight of all ... (they may) fly away from the sick,
and, destroying the disease which they had
produced, restore men to their former state."[59]

[58]   The City Of God, Bk. X, ch. 16; Bk. 21, ch. 6; Bk. 22, ch. 10. Tr. by Henry
       Bettenson; Pelican Classics, London, 1972.
[59]   Op. cit. ch. 18

- ◆ thus the demons trick the onlookers into thinking they have power to heal the sick; from which they gain the "bribe" of worship and sacrifices - or so Tatian thought.

2. Two Impossible Things

Whatever ability the devil may have either to perform, or to simulate, miraculous deeds, never forget that there are two inescapable limitations placed on any demonic activity or satanic power (Jn 8:44):

- ◆ Satan cannot sustain truth, because he is a liar from the beginning.

- ◆ Satan cannot sustain life, because he is a murderer from the beginning.

Therefore anyone who clings to the truth and life that are in Christ need never fear the devil, but rather will walk in the joyous freedom and fullness of a child of God! (Jn 8:32,36)

CHAPTER FIVE

POSSESSION AND EXORCISM

Evil is always better than goodness in imagination. It has a dramatic character that goodness seems to lack.

- Malcolm Muggeridge.

Nothing is so beautiful and wonderful, nothing so full of sweet and perpetual ecstasy, as the good; no desert is so dreary, monotonous, and boring as evil. But with fantasy it is the other way round. Fictional good is boring and flat, while fictional evil is varied and intriguing, attractive, profound, and full of charm.

- Simone Weil.

There is something about evil that fires the imagination. It has a dramatic character that goodness seems to lack. Most of us prefer to watch a film full of action, conflict, and high emotion, than a pleasant story about a series of good deeds. Somehow, in fiction virtuous people lack colour and vitality, whereas the wicked are drawn in vivid hues, full of energy and drama. Even heroes, if they are to be appealing in fiction, or on the screen, must ape the ways of the wicked - they win their battles by turbulent conflict, by coercion and trickery, by out-smarting, and out-fighting, their foes.

How many TV programs do you watch, where the hero or heroine wins by gentle, forgiving, self- denying, patient love? No doubt there are some. But they are rarely high in the ratings!

Think of your own imagination. How easily you conjure sensual images; how readily they tumble into your mind, brightly hued, gripping, vibrant. What compelling power carnal fantasies have! They hypnotise, they transfix, they hold you in their spell. Insistent, strong, they stick like burrs, and it takes great effort to shake them out. Virtuous thoughts, however, are fragile. They seem bland. They lack muscle. How hard it is to call up a technicolour image of yourself doing good! Almost as soon as you have given it shape, it dissolves away again, and a wicked notion leaps to takes its place!

That same rudiment makes demons seem more fascinating and exciting, more sensational, than angels - or even God. It is always easier to write about hell than about heaven. The devil can be described with passion more readily than the Lord. John Milton, in his stunning epic Paradise Lost, yielded unconsciously to that elemental flaw.

If you have read the poem (as I hope you have), then your memory of Milton's description of Satan is sure to be more vivid than of his depiction of God. Douglas Bush writes -

> "Like any imaginative artist, (Milton) could deal better with bad than with good characters, and there has never been any question of the magnificence of Satan, who remains one of the towering figures of world literature. In fact, the poet succeeded so greatly ... that it has (ever since) been conventional to regard Satan as the real hero of the poem, to say that Milton unconsciously projected his own rebellious instincts into his nominal villain."[60]

Bush himself does not accept that conventional view. And it may be true that Milton's Satan is not a reflection of the poet's "own rebellious instincts". But there is little doubt, as William Blake said, that

---

[60]   The Portable Milton, Penguin Books, New York, 1982; pg. 19.

" ... Milton wrote in fetters when he wrote of Angels
and God, and at liberty when of Devils and Hell..."
(61)

There is a warning here for us. Don't be snared by a fascination
with evil. Be wary when you approach this matter of demon
possession and exorcism. It is easy to become rapt by the kingdom
of darkness, to crave access to its hidden lore, to yearn for
knowledge beyond what is revealed. That pit has been a fatal lure
for many teachers. Many books are available, filled with esoteric
"knowledge", titillating, enticing, sensational, pretending to present
biblical truth when all the time their authors have strayed from the
sober words of scripture.

God forbid this book should join those, on the ash heap of
deception. Three rules have guided me -

1.   Avoid being baited by the thrill of the dark realm, and
retain a cool detachment toward all that belongs to the devil. Paul's
gives a sound admonition -

*I want you to be wise about what is good, and
simple about what is evil (Ro 16:19).*

The Greek word translated "simple", has several meanings, among
them the idea of being untainted or artless. It describes a guileless
person, not worldly-wise, whose want of knowledge leaves his
goodness unsullied. A child-like person. His mind is not devious;
he has no yen to penetrate forbidden zones; he is content with an
uncomplicated view of life. Such a demeanour is not always
desirable. It may sometimes betray an immoral indifference to
great issues. But we should have no other mind when we approach
the infernal realm. Forbid the devil any power to stir your curiosity
beyond a desire to know what is surely affirmed in scripture. Leave

---

(61)   The Marriage Of Heaven And Hell, note too *"The Voice Of The Devil."*
Blake wrote about 120 years after Milton.

inquisitive conjectures to those who, perhaps unknowingly, crave delusion.

2. The Bible alone can protect you from fallacy, and keep you grounded in truth. Surmise that goes beyond scripture, doctrine based on mere experience, must be shunned. But there is solidity in the word of God. It is more alive than life; more tangible than the hard earth; wiser than the wise; and tougher than death. You cannot get lost if you stay within the boundaries of scripture. No lie can withstand the assault of its mighty truth. Let its ramparts be your defence and all the battering of the wicked one will be vain. How refreshing, when your mind is fuzzy from the images of this world, and your sensibilities dulled by its clamour, to turn to the Bible! At once the devil's camouflage and the world's disguises are swept away. Their abject sham is exposed. Suddenly, the kingdom of God becomes the only source of reality!

3. Many so-called cases of exorcism are spurious, being rather a result of

♦ fascination with the drama of exorcism, which leads people to clamour for the exorcist and often unconsciously to fabricate the expected signs of demonic attack. The exorcist too, may be equally charmed by the excitement of his role, the sense of power it gives him, and the elation of spirit a seeming victory brings. So (perhaps unwittingly) he encourages the people to produce the required manifestations - the cries and convulsions, the retching, the naming of demons, and the like. Such things are wrong.

♦ people seeking an opportunity for emotional release within an uninhibited environment. Under the spell of exorcism they can do or say anything without incurring any personal blame or accountability. For some people, that provides a deep release, even a needed therapy. But there are better and safer ways to achieve the same result.

♦ demonic deception, where a person is not actually possessed, but a demon scornfully absorbs for hours the energies of both the exorcist and his clients, thus keeping them from wiser service in the church.

♦ sexual frustration, where a woman may secretly yearn for the sound of a strong male voice speaking at her with great authority. The exorcist, barking commands at the demon, meets an emotional hunger in her that would otherwise remain unfulfilled. The same can occur when a woman ministers to a man, or when exorcist and client are both of the same sex. You should place a high premium in this ministry on wisdom and caution.

Does that mean there is no genuine ministry in the church of loosing people from demonic power? Of course not. Demons are real. Their attacks on men and women are real. And if the servants of Christ do not take authority and release the prisoners in Jesus' name, then those captives will be left without hope. I am saying only that all deliverance ministry must be conducted with restraint, and strictly within a biblical framework. So then -

I. WHAT DOES THE BIBLE TEACH?

Please pause here, open your Bible, and read Acts 19:13-20. Is that story a relic of ancient superstition? Hardly! The apostles themselves acted against superstition when they burned in the public square those scrolls on sorcery and magic. Is the story fiction? No. A forger could not have resisted the temptation to include an account of Paul loosing the demonised man with a single command (did you notice that the man ran away, and as far as we know, remained tormented?) So the story is true. Which raises a sharp question. How do you get a reputation like Paul had among demons? Do they tremble when they hear your name?

The key is knowledge. The demons said: "We know!" Therefore they had authority to resist the seven exorcists and to beat them severely. But those exorcists did not know; so they were helpless. Authority over demons depends upon knowing certain key things -

A. KNOW YOUR ENEMY

Augustine argued that *daimion* was derived from the word for knowledge. Demons, he said, are so called because they distort knowledge and use it sinfully. His etymology is probably wrong, but the idea is right.[62]

Victory over demons, then, begins with countermanding that corrupted knowledge, replacing it with the truth, and holding to that truth in love (cp. Ge 2:17; 3:1-7; Jn 8:31-32, 36). This should also remind you that possession is neither the worst nor the cleverest work of Satan. He is far more dangerous when he comes in pleasant dress, with fair lies, enticing wiles, and charming baubles.

The worst ignorance is false knowledge. Better not to know at all than to know wrongly. Who is so deceived as the man who, thinking it to be the truth, believes a lie? No delusion is more profound. The man who knows he does not know is open to learn; but folly imprisons him who thinks he does know.

So beware of accretions that cling to what the Bible teaches about the devil and demons. Those superfluous speculations cage people inside a fixed pattern of behaviour. This added "knowledge" imposes on them a set of rigid assumptions. They become locked into certain standard expectations. They build formulae, and rituals, and routines, heedlessly copying the incantations of the ancients. They prevent the free moving of the Holy Spirit. But the Lord cannot be confined by anything except scripture!

B. SOBERING PROPHECY

Two things especially you should know about your demonic foes, based on Re 13:7 ...

---

[62]   City Of God, Bk. 9, ch. 20 & 21.

1. They Make War On The Saints

I have warned you not to be unduly aware of demons, nor to focus too much attention on the kingdom of darkness. But there is a worse fault: to ignore altogether the satanic realm. There is war in the heavenlies. Whether we choose to be or not, you and I are involved in that cosmic battle. It rages all around us, never ceasing day or night. The earth itself is the front line. Here the mighty armies struggle for supremacy - although God has already decreed the outcome. Hence the devil's raging despair (Re 12:12).

So "be sober, be vigilant" (1 Pe 5;8), for the careless, the unheeding, will soon be overthrown.

Yet once again, let us call for balance. Despite the way people often talk, Satan himself has probably never attacked you. He is not God. He can be in only one place at a time. His knowledge and power are limited. It is unlikely that you and I are important enough to warrant his personal attention! In scripture, the word Satan can be a metonym for any part of the dark domain - just as we might say "Washington", but mean the government of the USA, or any of its agents. If the devil attacks you, it is more likely through one his servants than by his own hand.

Even so, you might live your whole life and never be overtly attacked by a demon, especially if Satan knows in advance the attack would be futile. Remember, demons are finite in number and limited in mobility. Presumably their present number is fixed, and cannot be increased. They must travel from point to point (Mt 12:43-45).[63] They cannot go where God forbids them. Their

---

[63] Tertullian expresses a quaint contrary view, holding that demons can move so swiftly they are virtually omnipresent. His argument is unconvincing; but judge for yourself -

"Every spirit is possessed of wings. This is a common property of both angels and demons. So they are everywhere in a single moment; the whole world is as one place to them; all that is done over the whole extent

wisdom is corrupt. They bear heavy chains of divine judgment (Mt 8:29).

By contrast, the population and wisdom of mankind (particularly the church) are constantly increasing. So it seems improbable there are enough demons to provide a troop around every person. More likely the devil must conserve his forces, shooting only at vulnerable targets; or perhaps he contents himself with an occasional skirmish against each of us, when he senses a chance of success.

So we are involved in warfare. This conflict is not so fierce as some have claimed, but more fierce than others say it is, and for most of us its personal intensity waxes and wanes. Because the conflict is real, we should walk prudently. Because the triumph of Christ is great, we should walk victoriously!

2. They Can Overcome The Saints

God has allowed the princes of evil to "make war on the saints and to conquer them" (Re 13:7). That is one of the most arresting statements in the Bible. Our minds tell us it ought not to be so. How can God give the enemy such freedom against his own holy people? Yet both scripture and experience confirm the fact. Why does God allow it? To that, there is no full answer this side of the resurrection, although you may remember some of the suggestions I made in Chapter One.

But whether we understand it or not, the conflict is real, and the casualties many. What form does the enemy's assault take? As I have suggested just above, while his onslaught may sometimes take a direct form, more commonly it is indirect. He strives to overthrow you through his malign influence over our whole society and culture.

---

of it, it is as easy for them to know as to report. Their swiftness of motion is taken for divinity, because their nature is unknown ... " Apology, ch. 22. Op. cit.

But there are some exceptions, the most notable being: demonic trespass upon a person (usually called "possession"); and infliction of disease and premature death.

II. DEMON POSSESSION

Forgive me if I weary you by stressing again that anyone who approaches the subject of demon possession claiming to have all the answers is either a simpleton, a deceiver, or an irresponsible teacher. Anyone who has seriously examined all the data knows that mystery shrouds the subject of demonology.

It is impossible finally to define the nature of demon possession; it is impossible finally to say who can or who can't be demon-possessed; it is impossible to determine the degree of risk of possession confronting a person at any particular time; it is impossible to ascertain the real prevalence of demon possession in our present society; and so on.

The evidence given in the NT enable us to assert only two things about demon possession: first, the phenomenon is real, not imaginary; second, through the triumph of Christ, every believer has both authority over every demon and the right to deliverance from all demonic oppression.

III. THE NATURE OF DEMON POSSESSION

A. WHAT ARE DEMONS?

Just as the four great western world religions (Zarathustrianism, Judaism, Christianity, Islam) believe in a hierarchy of angels, so they believe in a hierarchy of demons. According to the three latter faiths, the hierarchy culminates in Satan, the sole monarch of the dark realm. There is no biblical reason to doubt that picture. But perhaps one falsehood should be corrected. I hope you have banished from your mind the fiction that "hell" (the place of punishment for the damned) is the place of Satan's throne. The popular myth of the devil and his minions ruling over hell and assisting in the torment of lost souls, is a fairy tale. The first victim incarcerated in hell will in fact be Satan (along with the "Beast" and the "False Prophet"). It is his place of anguish, not authority (Re 20:10).

Other aspects of popular mythology may be equally wrong. For example: the idea that Satan was an archangel who led a third of the angels into rebellion against God. Michael and the holy angels (it is said) suppressed the revolt and cast Satan and his legions out of heaven. In the process, Satan became the devil, and the fallen angels became demons. That may be what happened, but scripture is silent on the matter.[64]

Perhaps the only reason to accept the myth is its hoary antiquity. For example, the 7th century monk Caedmon, one of the earliest English Christian poets, told the story this way -

> The fiend with all his comrades
> Fell then from heaven above,
> Through as long as three nights and days,
> The angels from heaven into hell;
> And them all the Lord transformed to devils,
> Because they his deed and word
> Would not revere.[65]

---

[64]   There is, of course, an account of a heavenly war in Re 12:7-10. But nothing in that passage identifies Satan with an archangel, nor the ruined angels with demons.

[65]   Creation: *The Fall Of The Rebel Angels*. Caedmon was a poor, illiterate herdsman, until he claimed to have seen a vision, in which he was commanded to sing the creation story of Genesis. Soon, as if divinely inspired, he began turning Bible stories into simple but vigorous verse. He was eventually admitted by the monks at Whitby Abbey as an honoured member to their order. (Wycliffe Biographical Dictionary of the Church).

Whatever they are, wherever they come from, demons remain real, and their attacks on men and women wreak great havoc. But that raises an important question: just how do demons attack people?

B. POSSESSED OR OPPRESSED?

Is there any difference between demonic possession and oppression? The question is significant, because some people argue that Christians may be oppressed by the devil, but not possessed by him. Only the ungodly, they say, can be truly possessed. I will examine below the arguments used to support this belief; but first let us see how the NT uses these terms.

Notice that the Greek text does not distinguish between possessed and oppressed. The apostles used two generic expressions, both of which have a wide significance -

    1. To be "demonised" *(daimonidzomai)*

More than any other word, the gospel writers used *daimonidzomai* to describe demonic attack - Mt 4:24; 8:16,28,33; 9:32; 12:22; 15:22; Mk 1:32; 5:15,16,18; Lu 8:36; Jn 10:21.

To be "demonised" means to be under the control or influence of a demon, mentally, spiritually, or physically. The degree of "demonisation" may vary immensely from case to case - from slight influence to total control. The word itself does not demand the idea of complete possession, nor does it forbid that idea.

    2. To be "oppressed" *(katadunasteuo)*

The single occurrence of this verb in the NT (connected with the work of Satan), is significant. Luke uses it to summarise Christ's entire ministry of deliverance -

God anointed Jesus of Nazareth with the Holy Spirit and with power; and he went about doing good and healing all that were oppressed by the devil, for God was with him (Ac 10:38).

Katadunasteuo means "to have power over, to tyrannise, to oppress". Again, this word leaves unspecified the degree or kind of oppression the person may be suffering. It may describe everything from light affliction to absolute control; it may include any kind of sickness or trouble, spiritual, mental, or physical.

3. Alternative Expressions

The NT uses several other expressions to describe various demonic attacks. These words all seem to have a general rather than a specific sense - that is, they are all more or less interchangeable, and different writers freely use them to describe situations that are virtually identical:

- ♦ to "have" a demon: Mt 11:18; Mk 7:25; 9:17; Lu 4:33; 7:33; 8:27; Jn 7:20; 8:49; 10:20; Ac 8:7; 16:16.

- ♦ to be "with" a demon: Mk 1:23; 5:2.

- ♦ to be "taken" by a demon: Lu 9:39.

- ♦ to be "tormented" by a demon: Lu 6:18; Ac 5:16.

- ♦ to be "seized" by a demon: Lu 8:29.

Demoniacs are also called the "dwelling place" of a demon (Mt 12:45; Lu 11:26), and a number of demons can dwell in one person at the same time (Mt 12:45; Mk 5:9; Lu 8:2).

This lack of precision in terminology shows that the NT writers were unaware of, or not interested in, the kinds of fine distinctions many modern teachers make. They did not draw a line between possession and oppression. They acknowledged that demonic attacks took various forms, and that some forms were more terrible than others, but they did not make any special effort to distinguish between these forms. They saw them all as attacks of Satan, which should be resisted and overcome in the authority of Christ.

This brings us to the real heart of the matter: the NT writers did not write about demons at all, they wrote about Christ. Demons were mentioned only because Christ came into conflict with them and overcame them. The emphasis in the gospels is clear: one of Christ's chief works on earth was to shatter demonic power once and for all - Mk 1:24; Lu 4:31; 1 Jn 3:8; etc. Everywhere Jesus encountered demons he proved to be stronger than they.

Whenever the NT mentions demons, whether they are duelling with Jesus or with his disciples, they are portrayed as defeated, terrified, on the run. The disciples found that their mastery over demons was like that of Jesus: complete! (Mt 10:1; Mk 3:15; 6:7,13; 9:38; Lu 9:1,49; 10:17-18; Ac 8:7; 19:12).

After the day of Pentecost, whenever they were engaged in deliverance ministry, the disciples experienced no prolonged struggle, nor any uncertainty about the outcome. Apparently they took little notice of the way expelled demons left the people from whom they had been cast - or if they did, they left us no record of their observations. In fact, the problems faced by many modern exorcists, and the issues that seem to fascinate many modern writers on the subject, were unknown to the first Christians. This is perhaps the main reason why the NT data on demonology are so sparse. Because their mastery over demons was so great, and because they loosed the demon- possessed with such little difficulty, the apostles had no reason to research the matter further.

Perhaps the speculations, curiosity, struggles, frustrations, bizarre manifestations, and the like, which so consume the energies of many modern exorcists, simply reflect their loss of the authority held by the early church. Such things may also reflect a wrong method, based on a false understanding of the manner in which demons are active in the world.

4.   When Demons Prevailed

There are two instances in the NT when demons refused to leave those whom they had possessed. The first is the case of the epileptic boy (Mt 17:14-21; Mk 9:14-29; Lu 9:37- 43); the second is the case of the Jewish exorcists (Ac 19:13-16). The latter story presents no difficulties, for the sons of Sceva had no proper spiritual authority to expel demons, and their beating at the hands of the demoniac was inevitable. But what about the apparent failure of the disciples to heal the epileptic boy? Surely this shows that sometimes exorcism requires a long struggle, and that defeat is occasionally inevitable?

Note first, whatever was the cause of the disciples' failure in this instance, this was not their ordinary experience. They learned the lesson well, and enjoyed stunning success in their later missions (as they had already done in earlier missions) - compare Lu 9:1 with verses 40-42, and then see 10:17; Ac 5:16.

Second, notice that Jesus was quite impatient with the disciples' failure, and allowed them no excuse for it (Mt 17:17; Mk 9:19; Lu 9:41). He expected his disciples to expel the demon as easily as he himself did. Ignoring the boy's convulsive frenzy, Jesus spoke only a few words of command, and at once the evil spirit left the child, and he was completely healed. All three synoptists record this story in some detail; which shows the disciples' determination that the lesson should not be forgotten. Such an embarrassing defeat must never occur again!

The story also shows the reaction the ascended Christ must have to the kind of fruitless and frustrating sessions of exorcism I have often read about or witnessed. When the practice of deliverance, and the measure of success enjoyed, drifts as far away from the NT paradigm as it has in many parts of the church today, then surely it is time to stop. Questions should be asked about the concepts underlying much modern practice. Why continue with an ineffective, or unbiblical, practice? Is faith truly present? The words of Jesus, and the example of the NT, surely tell us this: where true faith is present, and when right methods built on good doctrine are employed, delivering the demonised from their afflictions ought to be an easy part of Christian ministry.

There is nothing in the NT to encourage surrounding deliverance ministry with the extravagant and repulsive behaviour often observed today. One could accept these odd manifestations, this aberrant conduct, if results commensurate with those of the NT were gained. But when neither NT practice is followed, nor NT results seen, then it is time to stop, and to seek new understanding and new direction.

I will return to exorcism later; but we should pause here and ask where we have gone so far. We have discovered three things -

a. While the NT does not attempt to answer questions about the origin, nature, and methods of demons, it does present a vivid picture of an unseen and spirit-world that is fiercely opposed both to Christ and the church. Mystery surrounds the existence of that spirit-world; but we know enough to accept its reality, and to combat its influence.

b. Christ triumphed through the cross; therefore the kingdom of darkness is now subservient to his will. This complete dominion has been delegated to the church -

> *Behold, I have given you authority to tread upon serpents and scorpions, and over all the power of the enemy; and nothing shall hurt you" (Lu 10:19).*

Christ expects his church to use its authority, not only to maintain its own security but also to deliver those who are oppressed by the devil (Mt 10:1; Mk 3:15; 6:7,13; 16:17; Lu 9:1).

c. Those who are in any way controlled or afflicted by demons are spoken of as being "demonised", whether or not the demon may be thought of as dwelling inside them, or as outwardly attacking them. It is doubtful if the semantics of demon possession held any interest for the NT writers. It seems foolish to build doctrines on expressions that are not even used, let alone defined, in the NT. Hence, it is futile to argue about whether a person is possessed, obsessed, oppressed, influenced, or the like. Such words may be useful to illustrate various degrees of "demonisation"; but they become erroneous when they are used to bolster arguments about who can, or cannot, be actually "possessed" by a demon.

Which raises the question -

C. CAN A CHRISTIAN BE DEMON-POSSESSED?

1. A Question Of Semantics

A brief answer would be: take the semantics away and the problem ceases to exist. If you use the two major NT words (demonised and oppressed) in their ordinary broad sense, you will see at once that Christians can be attacked and afflicted (even "overcome", Re 13:7) by the devil.

To the NT writers, the question about whether or not this "demonisation" or "oppression" extends to what some call "possession", would have been a non-issue. Our concept of demon-possession (a particular category of demonisation, distinct from any other) had no place in their thinking. They did not recognise different kinds of demonisation, only different degrees, and even then they probably did not construct any formal definitions. The NT writers dealt with demons only in the process of recording things that had actually happened. The theory behind such events did not interest them. They were building a doctrine of Christ, not a doctrine of devils (cp. 1 Ti 4:1), and they had no room to speculate about dark powers whom they saw as already thoroughly routed by Christ. So the question in NT days would not have been, "Can a Christian be demon- possessed?" but rather, "Can a Christian be demonised?" And to this, the answer would have been, "Yes!"

However, some would claim that I am still begging the question. Can a Christian be actually indwelt, or "possessed", by a demon, in the modern meaning of the term. To that question, despite what I have written above, they would return a resounding, "No!"

Following are some quotes from well-known Christian leaders. I am leaving them un-named, because I do not wish (on such a sensitive issue) either to endorse or condemn any particular servant of the Lord. The writers quoted are all devout men, internationally known, and their beliefs command respect

2. Some Contrary Opinions

"I see this spurious doctrine of demonised Christians ripping the Body of Christ to pieces."

"I have no controversy with exorcism in unbelievers, but I must reject the doctrine that says demons can inhabit Christians who are truly born of the Spirit. Recent books and articles which teach this are the most faith- destroying and fear-inspiring perversions I have ever read."

"The Bible makes it positively clear that he who is born of God cannot be ruled or possessed by Satan. And yet we have a growing number of people today who live in constant fear of lurking demons, ready to inhabit their holy temples ... There is now an alarming emphasis on demons and Satan in charismatic circles. The neo-demonism prevalent today suggests Christians can be inhabited by as many as 300 demons. Every problem, every human failure, every disease, every habit, is attributed to direct demon influence ... (People) blame all their trouble and weakness on a `demon' making them do things against their will, and they seek out an exorcist who can, with a single prayer of dominion, end their battle ... (Yet) Satan cannot possess any person who has been born of God! Demons cannot enter a blood-washed child of Christ! Those who teach otherwise base their doctrine only on human experience. They cannot prove it from the scripture at all! ... (Satan) cannot enter a Christian unless he first binds the Christ in him and casts Him out ... The Christian is warned by God's Word to beware of the devices of Satan. But Jesus always distinguished between devices, torments, and possession by demons. **They are not the same.**" (Emphasis from the original author.)

The latter quote is a peculiar mixture of fact and fancy. I share the author's dislike of the practice of blaming the devil for all sorts of personal troubles. I share also his suspicion of claims that several hundred demons have been cast out of some people. [66] I agree with him that much of the current "neo-demonism" is unscriptural and harmful. Thoughtful people should reject such perilous practices. But then his own credibility is made doubtful by such sweeping claims as, "Jesus always distinguished between devices, torments, and possession by demons." He quotes Mt 4:24 to establish this surprising claim - a passage which says only that Jesus healed "demoniacs" (literally, the demonised), along with many other people who were afflicted with "various diseases and pains, epileptics, and paralytics". I have not been able to find any place in the gospels where Jesus so much as suggests that there are different forms of "demonisation", some of which can, and some which cannot, afflict the children of God. But then, I have observed that the protagonists on both sides of this quarrel are often stronger in assertions than they are in careful proof.

[66] The gospel writers were awed by the fact that just seven demons were cast out of Mary Magdalene (Mk 16:9; Lu 8:2), and they drew special attention to it as a remarkable miracle. They were also amazed by the unique and incredible case of Legion (Mk 5:1- 13; and cp. Mt 8:28-33; Lu 8:26-33). All three synoptists record this story, and they agree that Legion (and his partner?) had "many" demons - but he was also a madman possessing supernatural strength. The manner in which these stories are told shows they were exceptional cases, and that such multiple possession is rare. Note also, the number of demons in Legion is not specified; we are simply told they were "many". Mark says that 2000 swine rushed into the sea, and perished; but that does not prove there were 2000 demons. If only a few members of the herd were seized by a frenzy it would be enough to panic the entire herd. Nor does the name "Legion" necessarily indicate a number of demons as large as a Roman army legion - for the name is defined by Legion himself as simply meaning "many".

3. A Strange Viewpoint

And now, one final quote -

> "What is the difference between demon possession
> and satanic oppression? Serious problems result
> from confusion on this point. Simply stated,
> possession is demonic, while oppression is satanic.
> The former is an attack from the inside; the latter is
> an attack from the outside. Satan does not inhabit
> the human body. Jesus never cast Satan out of
> anyone, but he did cast demons out of those who
> were possessed ... In demon possession, the victim
> is dominated, body, soul, and spirit, by an evil
> spirit, and is helpless to effect his own deliverance.
> I can find no Scriptural evidence to show that an
> obedient believer in Jesus can be possessed by a
> demon ... On the other hand, satanic oppression is a
> very real problem among God's children. We are
> never told to resist demons, because they have no
> power over the child of God."

That paragraph comes from a book with whose general meaning I
am in agreement. Its author rightly opposes the immense harm
done by incautious demonologies and by irresponsible exorcists.
But while I agree with the broad purpose of the book, I cannot
endorse the style of argument it uses. The writer's "proofs" are as
insubstantial as those he opposes.

The paragraph quoted is typical of much of the book. The author
says: "Possession is demonic, while oppression is satanic." But he
is just playing games with words. It is a verbal juggler's trick,
lacking any valid biblical support. He adds: "The former is an
attack from the inside, the latter is an attack from the outside" How
impossible to establish that claim from scripture! Such
unsupported assertions prove nothing, except that the author has
already made up his mind what he wants to say, and will say it,
regardless of whether he can find scriptural proof. He continues:

"In demon possession, the victim is dominated, body, soul, and spirit, by an evil power and is helpless to effect his own deliverance." That may be true for the author's pre-conceived idea of what demon possession is like; but it has no likeness to NT descriptions of people who were "demonised". Yet it is true, alike for those who argue for demonised Christians as for those who argue against it, lack of NT data on which to build a strong case, compels them to fabricate their own evidence. Careful students should admit this: there is simply insufficient information in scripture to enable anyone to construct a clear and precise demonology.

He claims: "I can find no scriptural evidence to show that an obedient believer in Jesus can be possessed by a demon." That may be true, but neither is there any evidence to show that such a person cannot be demon possessed.

He concludes: "We are told, `Resist the devil ... ' We are never told to resist demons, because they have no power over the life of a child of God."

True, we are offered a place of marvellous strength in God, so that we fear nothing that belongs to the kingdom of darkness. But to say that Christians are fully immune from demonic attack surely claims too much - cp. Ro 8:37-39; 2 Co 12:7; Ep 6:11,16.

4. A Limited Being

Satan is a finite being, able to be only in one locality at one time. How could he personally afflict or tempt millions of people every hour of every day? Remember my earlier suggestion: many of the occurrences of "the devil" or "Satan" in the NT must be seen as metonymy or synecdoche, that is, describing one thing in terms of another, or using a part to refer to the whole. An example: saying "David defeated the Philistines," but meaning the battle was won by the whole army of Israel, which was merely led by David; or, referring to "Caesar", when in fact the Roman government was meant. Likewise, many verses that speak only of Satan should be taken to include his entire kingdom and all the agents who are under his control.

Can I prove that? Easily! See the following:

- ♦ Ac 10;38. The gospels show that demons were part of the action described as being "oppressed by the devil".

- ♦ Ac 26:18. Even our author would allow that the ungodly are troubled by demons as well as by Satan. But if demons are part of the statement here, then there is no reason to exclude them from similar statements elsewhere.

- ♦ Ro 16:20. Are not demons "under our feet", as well as Satan?

- ♦ 1 Co 5:5. Was his satanic majesty really involved personally in this case, or does "Satan" actually mean one or more of his agents?

- ♦ 1 Co 7:5; 2 Co 2:11; 4:4; 11:14; 12:7 (surely a demon was in some way involved here?); Ep 2:2-3; 4:26-27; 6:11; 1 Th 3:5; 1 Ti 1:20; 2 Ti 2:26; Ja 4:7; 1 Pe 5:8; 1 Jn 2:13.

D. A MIDDLE CHOICE

1. Keep To The Scriptures!

If I keep to what is stated in the NT, avoiding both speculation and doubtful inference, then it is impossible to assert strongly either that Christians can or cannot be demon-possessed. If I were obliged to choose one position or the other, then I would opt for the negative choice. Why? Because it prevents the fanaticism and extremism prevalent among those who place a major emphasis on demonism in the church. It also has another virtue: it drives troubled people to prayer, to the word of God, and to an affirmation of their rights in Christ; thus it prevents them from seeking an easy (and false) solution to their burdens at the hands of an exorcist.

Happily, scripture does not demand from me such a hard choice. A compassionate pastor is free to minister to his people at whatever level wisdom requires. Some should be compelled to stand up and use their own spiritual authority; but others may sorely need their pastor to exercise authority on their behalf and to cast the evil one out of (or away from) them.

2. Points To Ponder

Here is an outline of some significant arguments against those who say that Christians cannot be demon-possessed -

a. If Christians cannot be demon-possessed, then every time demon- possessed people were converted to Christ their demons would have to leave them immediately. But then, the ministry of deliverance would vanish. It would be much easier, and more effective, simply to preach the gospel and win the demon-possessed to Christ.

Someone may retort that demon-possessed people are incapable of accepting the gospel. But that would add a deep spiritual bondage to the state of demon-possession that is not shown in the NT. Many demonised people described in the gospels were nothing more than physically afflicted - blind, dumb, diseased, and the like - they were not suffering any inescapable spiritual restraint. They were free to, and did, believe the gospel. Yet scripture says nothing about conversion by itself healing their various afflictions.

b. The link between demons and disease (which is discussed more fully below) seems to open the possibility of Christians being demonised. Particular diseases are sometimes attributed to demons, and sometimes not; the demonised are sometimes delivered by exorcism, but at other times by an act of "healing" (*therapeuo*).

c. Unless it is denied that Ananias was ever a Christian, the use of the same Greek word for "filled" in Ac 5:3

and Ep 5:18 would indicate that this man, a believer, had become deeply demonised (and cp. 1 Ti 4:1; and Lu 22:3).

      d. As indicated above, many references to "Satan" should be taken in a generic sense to include the entire kingdom of darkness. Therefore, since scripture is unequivocal about the devil attacking Christians, they must also be subject to sore attack by demonic "principalities and "powers".

It is a mistake either to maximise or minimise the devil's power to attack a Christian, whether personally, or by some demonic agency. The extremism of both ends of the argument should be avoided. The mere assertion of a doctrine cannot alter reality. If people are demonised, they need deliverance, whether or not some doctrine agrees with this; and if they are not demonised, then no doctrine can magically plant a demon in them. This is one area where mere theory ought to yield to apparent human need.

      3. For Your Interest

There are numerous references to exorcism in the writings of the Church Fathers. Here for your interest are two of them, which show the belief of the early church that Christians can be demonised -

> "We have the woman (the Lord himself is my witness) who went to the theatre, and came back possessed. Later, during exorcism, when the unclean creature was upbraided with having dared to attack a believer, he firmly replied: `I was certainly within my rights, for I came upon her while she was in my domain' ... What nobler than to tread underfoot the gods of the nations - to exorcise

evil spirits - to perform healings - to seek divine revelations - to live for God?" [67]

"For we forewarn you to be on your guard (against) those demons ... (lest they should) deceive you ... For they strive to hold you their slaves and servants; and sometimes by appearances in dreams, and sometimes by magical impositions, they subdue all who make no strong opposing effort for their own salvation."[68]

IV. DEMONS AND DISEASE

For mysterious and uncertain reasons (apart from their desire to ravage mankind) demons seem to be under a compelling necessity to possess a human body (Lu 11:24), in fact any kind of body (Mk 5:12). Without such a possession they are restless and destitute. Hence they constantly seek a "house" in which to dwell. Their "possession" of this human dwelling often results in diseases of many sorts.

Four things are noteworthy about the biblical approach to this matter: first, the Bible does not hesitate to attribute many human ailments to demonic invasion; second, the Bible is equally emphatic that not all sickness should be linked with a demon; third, a particular sickness may sometimes be caused by a demon, but may also be distinguished from demonisation; fourth, a demonised person may remain well physically, but show in other ways the presence of a demon -

---

[67]   Tertullian, The Shows, ch. 26 & 29. Op. cit. The whole story in ch. 26 is worth reading.

[68]   Justin Martyr, Apology, 1.14. Ibid.

A. EVIDENCE FROM THE NEW TESTAMENT

1. The Bible Links Disease And Demonisation

The following diseases are specifically attributed to demonisation: mental derangement (Mt 8:24-34; Lu 8:26-35; Mk 5:1-20); dumbness (Mt 9:32-34; 12:22-30; Mk 9:17-26; Lu 11:14); blindness (Mt 12:22-30); epilepsy (Mt 17:14-21; Mk 9:17-29; Lu 9:37-43).

There are also instances where "healing" occurred after the expulsion of a demon, but the disease remains unspecified (Mt 4:24; 15:21-28; Lu 4:40-41; 6:18; 7:21; 8:2; 13:10-13,16; etc.).

Also, the way in which the sick and the demonised are so frequently referred to in the same context shows the close association between demonic power and disease.

2. The Bible Distinguishes Between Disease and Demonisation

They brought him all the sick, those afflicted with various diseases and pains, demoniacs, epileptics, and paralytics, and he healed them" (Mt 4:24).

That verse separates demonised from diseased people; in other words, Matthew did not think every sick person was demonised. The apostles recognised that many diseases were physical in their origin; therefore it would be foolish to see a demon lurking behind every ailment. This distinction is shown in Mt 8:17; 10:1,8; Mk 1:32-34; 6:13; Lu 6:17-18; 7:21; 9:1; 13:32; Ac 5:16; 8:7; 19:12.

Physical sickness, of course, may have been part of the demonised state of at least some of those people; but a difference is still drawn between them and those who were diseased yet not demonised.

In the OT, sickness was sometimes attributed to satanic power, but more often it was not: Ge 48:1; 1 Kg 14:1; 17:17; 2 Kg 1:2; 8:7; 13:14; 20:1; Da 8:27; and cp. Sir 31:2. The NT also speaks of many who were sick without suggesting they were demonised: Mt 8:14; Ac 9:33,37; 28:8; Ph 2:26; 2 Ti 4:20. It also lists many diseases and distinguishes them from demon possession: lunacy, paralysis, dumbness, deafness, leprosy, fever, blindness, haemorrhage, and so on. Admittedly, the link in the NT between demons and disease is strong, and there is an expectation that where you find one you may well find the other; but the early Christians were still well aware that demons and disease are not always associated with each other.

The apostles, then, did not use demons as a convenient way to explain why people became sick. They did not reckon every misery to be the work of some demon. Ignorance, superstition, or fear, were not the basis for their belief in demons. On the contrary, their understanding of the real nature of things was quite sophisticated. They well knew how to discriminate between natural and preternatural forces. A critic may disagree with the opinion of the early church on these matters, but he cannot fairly accuse the first Christians of being naive simpletons who believed in demons because they knew no better.

3. A Given Disease May Or May Not Be Demonic

Here is a remarkable thing about the demonology of the gospels: sometimes they attribute a particular sickness to demons; while on other occasions no demon is involved. Even more startling is the difference in healing methods employed in each case. For example, look at two deaf mutes (one a man, the other a boy) healed by Christ. The boy was demonised; the man was not.

"A deaf and dumb spirit" possessed the demonised boy, and was the direct cause of his affliction. Jesus healed him by sternly rebuking the evil spirit and forcibly expelling it (Mk 9:25-26). But natural causes were apparently the source of the man's deafness and muteness. Here there was no rebuke, no convulsion, no violent reaction, no angry command. With gentle sympathy Jesus took him aside privately, softly touched his ears and his tongue, and with one word, *Eph'phatha*, instantly cured his deafness and his dumbness. How astonished the people were! They cried, "He

(Jesus) has done all things well; he even makes the deaf hear and the dumb speak!" (Mk 7:31-37).

Likewise, blindness is sometimes attributed to demons (Mt 12:22), but sometimes not (Lu 7:21). And the same is true of epilepsy (cp. Mt 4:24 with 17:15,18).

Another group of references provides further support. They describe diseases that elsewhere are attributed to demons, but which here do not seem to have any demonic origin - cp. Mt 11:5; 15:29-31; 21:14 (however, it is fair to point out that Lu 7:21-23 does mention "evil spirits").

Even if the meaning of some of the references I have quoted is uncertain, there are still enough to show that the early Christians had more wisdom than numerous modern exponents of demonology. Some of these contemporary exorcists have everything wonderfully categorised. They know exactly which sickness or symptom is demonic, and which is not. The early Christians showed much better sense. They were wary of tidy compartments. They took each case on its merits. They knew that one demonised mute did not mean every mute was demonised. We need to pray that God will give us the same careful discrimination.

4. The Demonised Are Not Always Diseased

While sickness may be a common result of demonic attack, it is not always so, and people can be demonised without becoming physically ill or infirm. They may not even be adversely affected mentally - on the contrary, their perceptions may be sharpened (cp. Mk 3:11-12; etc). The gospels describe people who were not obviously ill, who may have been full of vigour and enjoying excellent health, yet were possessed by one or more evil spirits. They were "possessed" morally, or spiritually, rather than physically, (cp. Mk 1:21-28; Lu 4:33-37; 6:18; Ac 8:16- 19; 19:12).

What was true in Bible days is presumably true today: some sick people are demonised, but others are not; a particular disease may result from natural causes, or it may have a demonic origin; some demonised people show the effect in their bodies, but in other cases the effect is seen in their mental, moral, emotional, or spiritual condition; and so on.

Who is adequate to bring deliverance to the oppressed? I suppose only those who are mature in understanding, strong in faith, bold in heart, and liberally endowed with the "ability to distinguish between spirits" (1 Co 12:10).

B. THE TESTIMONY OF THE FATHERS

1. They never hesitated to associate demons with disease -

"We are instructed ... from our sacred books, how from certain angels, who fell of their own free will, there sprang a more wicked demon-brood ... Their great business is the ruin of mankind ... They inflict accordingly upon our bodies diseases and other grievous calamities ... Very kind too, no doubt, they are in regard to the healing of diseases. For, first of all, they make you ill; then, to get a miracle out of it, they command the application of remedies either altogether new, or contrary to those in use, and straightway withdrawing hurtful influence, they are supposed to have wrought a cure ... "[69]

"There are, indeed, diseases and disturbances of the matter that is in us, and, when such things happen, the demons ascribe the causes of them to themselves, and approach a man whenever disease lays hold of him. Sometimes they themselves disturb the habit of the body by a tempest of folly;

---

[69] Tertullian, Apology, ch. 22. Ibid. Chapters 21, 22, & 23 comprise a rather complete picture of Tertullian's demonology, a mixture of shrewd insight with dashes of gullibility.

but, being smitten by the word of God, they depart
in terror, and the sick man is healed."[70]

So demons sometimes inflicted sickness, while at other times they took advantage of the onset of disease. But while the Fathers knew we could not escape involvement in the warfare between heaven and the devil's armies, they also knew there was necessity for us to be overcome in that war. In the name of Jesus, victory is assured!

---

[70] Tatian, To The Greeks, ch. 16. Op. Cit.

CHAPTER SIX

EXORCISM

When I remember some of the wild and foolish things I have seen zealous exorcists do over the years, I almost wish the Roman Catholic rubric might become mandatory for the whole church -

> "A priest may not perform an exorcism without special authorisation of his bishop, and such authorisation is to be granted only to a cleric noted for his piety, prudence, and moral integrity. Before proceeding with an exorcism, the priest must make a careful and thorough investigation to determine whether or not he has to deal with a case of real possession."[71]

Look behind that rule and you will see irresponsible and extravagant practices like those that bedevil the charismatic movement today. Sometimes it is difficult to determine who is more overwrought, the exorcist or his (dare I say it?) victim. They are both screaming, sweating, and frothing!

Exorcism may sometimes be violent (Mk 9:26; Lu 4:35), noisy (Ac 8:7; Lu 9:39), even dramatic; but never fanatical. Biblical exorcists never surrendered their dignity - except perhaps when they failed! (Cp. Mk 9:18-19; Ac 19:13-17). Where genuine faith and true spiritual mastery exist, there will be no prolonged and repetitious rebuking and commanding; there will be no loss of control over what is happening. Jesus could not prevent the boy from going into

---

[71]   Encyclopaedia Britannica, Vol. 8, pg. 300. 1963 edition.

a convulsion and screaming; but his mastery over the situation was never threatened. Before anyone had time to be offended, or terrified, the lad was delivered and restored to his joyful father.

According to the gospels and Acts, when the disciples set themselves to cast out demons, they usually enjoyed good results. Their success was nearly equal to Christ's, and almost as easily gained (cp. Lu 10:17-18; notice that this refers to the seventy-two, not the twelve apostles). There is no reason for our success to be any less, nor should it come in a different form. The NT paradigm of exorcism is quite adequate. It is certainly preferable to the bizarre figments contained in many modern writings.[72]

I. EXORCISM IN THE OT

William Congreve three centuries ago coined the phrase, "Music has charms to soothe a savage breast." David may not have

---

[72] I could quote many passages that are more pagan than Christian; but here is one example -

"A common manifestation occurs in the hands. The hands may become numb or tingle. Sometimes the fingers become extended or rigid. Demons that manifest themselves in these ways through the hands are usually demons of lust, suicide, or murder. Other types of evil spirits, especially those associated with wrong use of the hands, may also manifest themselves in this way. Sometimes it is helpful for the person to shake the hands vigorously in order to dislodge the spirits."

Is it necessary to say how heathen all of that is? Nothing in scripture supports such categorising. The passage reads like something pulled out of the ruins of a Canaanite temple. It is arbitrary and capricious, irresponsible and delusory.

It is perhaps possible that during exorcism the hands of some demonised persons might go stiff; but to formalise such a reaction, to link it with specific demons, to turn it into a method of exorcism, is frivolous nonsense.

expressed the idea so nicely, but he did put the charms of music to good use - 1 Sa 16:14- 23.

That story of an evil spirit being driven away from Saul by David's music is the only example of exorcism in the OT. Unhappily, this musical mode of exorcism was not always effective, not even for David, the sweetest of Israel's singers (cp. 18:10; 19:9). Trying to drive away Saul's evil spirit nearly cost the shepherd his life! Perhaps success depended more on the words that were sung than on the music that was played? Perhaps David was successful when he attacked the demon with words, but not so successful when he relied only on melody? We shall never know.

The apocryphal story of Tobit, which I have already mentioned in an earlier chapter, contains the next nearest reference to exorcism.

The Jewish historian Josephus, however, tells an interesting (though utterly improbable) story about Solomon -

> "Now the sagacity and wisdom which God had bestowed upon Solomon was so great, that he exceeded the ancients, insomuch that he was no way inferior to the Egyptians, who are said to have been beyond all men in understanding; nay, indeed ... God also enabled him to learn that skill which expels demons, which is a science useful and sanative to men ... And he left behind him the manner of using exorcisms, by which they drive away demons, so that they never return, and this method of cure is of great force unto this day ...

> " ... I have seen a certain man of my own country whose name was Eleazar, releasing people that were demoniacal in the presence of Vespasian, and his son, and his captains, and the whole multitude of his soldiers. The manner of the cure was this: he put a

ring that had a root of one of those sorts mentioned by Solomon to the nostrils of the demoniac, after which he drew out the demon through his nostril;[73] and when the man fell down immediately, he abjured him to return into him no more, making still mention of Solomon, and reciting the incantations which he composed.

"And when Eleazor would persuade and demonstrate to the spectators that he had such a power, he set a little way off a cup or basin full of water, and commanded the demon as he went out of the man to overturn it, and thereby to let the spectators know that he had left the man; and when this was done the skill and wisdom of Solomon was shown very manifestly."[74]

II. EXORCISM IN THE NT

A. THE MINISTRY OF JESUS

1. A Marvellous Authority

Jesus astonished the people by a display of power over evil spirits such as they had never before heard of nor seen (Mk :27). They were amazed, not only by his remarkable success, but even more by the stark simplicity of his method - he spoke just a few words, and at once the spirits obeyed him. This was indeed "a new teaching!" No other person had ever shown such spiritual

---

[73] Believe it or not, I have heard modern exorcists, as gullible as Josephus, commanding demons to go out of a person through his nostrils, or mouth, or ears, or hands, and even his feet!

[74] Antiquities, VIII.ii.5. The phenomenon of the cup is also paralleled by the expectations of many modern exorcists. They look for some such physical or material sign either of a demon's presence or of its expulsion.

authority. No other person had ever taught that mastery over the powers of darkness could be so simply gained. No other teacher had ever offered so fully and freely to transfer his authority to his disciples.

The Jews were familiar with the kind of wandering exorcists described by Josephus, who plied their trade with trickery and incantations. They expected these men to use divinations, runes, spells, charms, and the like. In fact, if artifice and magical display were lacking from these exorcisms, they were hardly thought to be genuine.

But Jesus was so different! There is no record that he even laid hands on any demonised person. He merely spoke to them; and then without great anger or passion. His rebuke was stern, but plain: "Be silent, and come out of him" (Mk 1:25). The uncluttered mastery exercised by Jesus stands in striking contrast to the methods used by many other exorcists, both ancient and modern.

2. A Strange Omission

Have you noticed that the gospel writers did not once use the word "exorcism" to describe the ministry of Jesus?[75]

This peculiar omission of the ordinary word for "exorcism" was possibly caused by a determination to distinguish the ministry of Jesus from that of every other contemporary exorcist. The apostles wanted to show that Jesus scorned the superstitions, fears, and sorcery that were then so prevalent (and that are hardly less so today).

A wide difference can also be seen between the gospels and the apocrypha. How soberly the apostles reported the exorcisms performed by Jesus! How unbelievable are the older stories of Raphael using reeking smoke to drive away Asmodeus, or

---

[75] The Greek verb *horkizo*, and its intensified derivative *exorkizo,* occur only in Mt 26:63; Mk 5:7; Ac 19:13; 1 Th 5:27.

Solomon concocting weird nostrums and spells! Christ healed the demonised, not by using some spectacular display of power, but by the authority given to him by his Father. And how great was that authority! One sharp word was sufficient to drive every demon out of the two men at Gadara - "Go!"[76]

Whenever the gospels show Jesus expelling demons with nothing more than a spoken command, they reveal two other things about Christ: his absolute dominion over the whole kingdom of darkness; and the method by which he enforced that dominion. But having established those two things, the gospels then hasten to add another incredible fact: Jesus is willing to transfer his full authority to his church. His disciples may now act in his name, so that their command will have the same authority as his!

However, before discussing this transferred power, one other question should be answered -

3. How Did It Happen?

How did the demons come out of the people who were delivered by Christ?

a. Sometimes the mere presence of Jesus was enough to cause a demon to manifest itself - perhaps by crying aloud (Mt 8:29; Mk 1:24; 3:11; 5:7; Lu 4:34); perhaps by more violent behaviour (Mk 9:20; Lu 4:35; 9:42). But this did not always happen. The gospels record many instances when Jesus came into the presence of demonised people without stirring a reaction from either the people or the demons - or at least, we are not told about any reaction.

b. Sometimes there was a violent reaction by a demon only when Christ commanded it to leave - "after crying out and

---

[76] Mt 8:32. The Greek word is *hupagete*. In his version of the story, Mark uses *exelthe* = "Come out!" (Mk 5:8). The same kind of sharp command is recorded by Luke (4:35). See also Mt 8:16; Mk 7:29; 9:25; Lu 9:42.

convulsing him terribly, the demon came out, and the boy was like a corpse" (Mk 9:26; also 1:26). But again, this was not always the case - indeed, the special attention drawn to the few recorded examples may indicate that such manifestations were unusual.

        c. In the majority of accounts, the gospels describe no manifestation except the desired result of healing. A common expression is simply, "Jesus healed the demoniacs". Perhaps the only evidence a demon had been expelled was an end to the sickness its presence had caused.

Thus people knew that the blind and dumb demoniac was delivered because he "spoke and saw" after Jesus "healed" him (Mt 12:22; see also Mt 4:24; 15:28; Lu 6:18; 7:21). It is probably wrong to be looking always for some dramatic sign that a demon is present in a person, or that it has left him. The only worthwhile sign of successful exorcism is evidence that the formerly demonised person is demonised no more. Anything else is irrelevant, if not mischievous. Manifestations should neither be sought nor encouraged (Jesus rebuked them), and should be overcome as soon as possible.

        d. How does a demon leave a person? Through his mouth, his hands, his flesh, or some other way?

The belief is common that demons leave through the mouth; but scripture offers no clue, either how demons are able to enter human beings, or how they leave them. A demonised person may cry out during exorcism. But that does not prove that a demon has gone out through his mouth. Let the ancients keep to themselves their superstition that evil spirits could enter and leave the human body only through one of its orifices. We need not share their credulity.

Even less should you endorse another modern folly: supposing that a congregation is safe from demon attack during an exorcism, only if the people close their eyes and block their ears! They will be safe if they are praying (with their eyes closed or open), if they are not unreasonably fearful, and if there is no special factor that would make any of them open to demonic attack -

Like a sparrow in its flitting, like a swallow in its flying, a curse that is causeless does not alight (Pr 26:2).

Let safety be found in the things revealed in scripture. There is still too much superstition and gullibility surrounding the practice of exorcism.

B. THE MINISTRY OF THE DISCIPLES

1. The Twelve

The disciples followed the example of exorcism set by Jesus. They understood that he had established a basic pattern for them to follow.

Two key words unlock the power of Jesus' ministry: "authority" (*exousia*), and "expel" (*ekballo*) -

> *"With authority he commands even the unclean spirits, and they obey him" (Mk 1:27) ... "What is this word? For with authority and power he commands the unclean spirits, and they come out!" (Lu 4:36).*

> *"They brought to him many who were possessed with demons; and he cast out the spirits with a word" (Mt 8:16; 31-32; 9:33; Mk 1:34; Lu 11:14; 13:32).*

> *Jesus gave the same double right to his disciples -*

> *"He appointed twelve, to be with him, and to ... have authority (exousia) to cast out (ekballo) demons" (Mk 3:14- 15; see also Mt 10:1; Lu 9:1).*

Just before sending them out, Jesus confirmed again the spiritual authority he had given to the twelve -

> *"And he called to him the twelve, and began to send them out two by two, and gave them authority over the unclean spirits ... So they went out ... and they cast out many demons ... " (Mk 6:7,13).*

Their mission was highly successful. They had received from Christ the same command he had received from his Father, to "cast out" demons. Christ had transferred to them the same authority he had received from the Father. They obeyed his commission, they used his authority, they copied his method, and they obtained the same results!

2. The Seventy-Two

But this authority to cast out demons in the same way Jesus himself had done was not restricted to the twelve apostles. The Lord extended it to a further seventy-two disciples, who enjoyed the same success as the twelve (Lu 10:1,9,17-20).

But perhaps that was as far as Jesus intended to go? No! For we read of another man who was neither one of the twelve, nor one of the seventy-two; he was a stranger to them all - yet he seized the authority of Christ and went about casting out demons (Mk 9:38; Lu 9:49). The apostles tried to stop him, but they were sharply rebuked -

> *Do not forbid him; for no one who does a mighty work in my name will be able soon after to speak evil of me ... He that is not against you is for you (Mk 9:39; Lu 9:50).*

Plainly, Christ was saying that his authority to cast out demons in the same way he himself had done was available to any disciple who had the boldness to take it up and use it in his name.

But perhaps this privilege was current only while Jesus was on earth? No! For prior to his return to heaven the Lord extended the commission to heal the sick and cast out devils. He gave it to his entire church, to continue until the end of this age (Mk 16:15- 19). The early Christians certainly understood this to be so -

> *They went forth and preached everywhere, while the Lord worked with them and confirmed the message by the signs that attended it (Mk 16:20).*

They brought the sick and those afflicted with demons, and they were all healed (Ac 5:16) ... Stephen, full of grace and power, did great wonders and signs among the people (6:8) ... Unclean spirits came out of many who were possessed, crying with a loud voice (8:7) ... I charge you in the name of Jesus Christ to come out of her, and the demon came out that very hour (16:18) ... Diseases left them and the evil spirits came out of them (19:120; and cp. Ro 8:37-39; 15:18-19; 16:20; Ep 6:10-12; Cl 2:15.)

Can there be any further doubt? Jesus intended his church until the end of the age to continue the ministry of deliverance that he began. He, and no other, is to be our model. We are to heal the demonised as he did, with simplicity and authority. Like our Master we should shun the trappings that the heathen, the superstitious, and the credulous, attach to exorcism.

Some other comparisons need to be made between the ministry of Jesus and -

C. THE MINISTRY OF THE CHURCH

1. The Work Of The Holy Spirit

Christ strongly denied that he had (as a man) any personal power over Satan or over the kingdom of darkness. He claimed rather that his spiritual authority came from the Holy Spirit -

> *"Jesus, full of the Holy Spirit ... was led by the Spirit ... And Jesus returned in the power of the Spirit ... `By the Spirit of God I cast out demons' ... God anointed Jesus of Nazareth with the Holy Spirit and with power, and he went about doing good and healing all that were oppressed by the devil, for God was with him" (Lu 4:1,14; Mt 12:28; Ac 10:38; and cp. Lu 11:20).*

By the power of the indwelling Spirit Jesus healed the sick and cast out demons. The same resource is available to us. By the Spirit we are to be *"clothed with power from on high" (Lu 24:49). The works Jesus did (indeed, greater works than these) we can do, because he has given us the Spirit (Jn 14:12-17)*. His promise is emphatic - *"You shall receive power when the Holy Spirit has come upon you" (Ac 1:8)*; and in that power the church gains authority to heal the sick and cast out demons (5:12-16). The Holy Spirit, functioning in the church, imparts gifts of faith, healing, miracles, and "discerning of (evil) spirits" (1 Co 12:9-10).

Those references show that a ministry of deliverance should be one of the major results of the church being filled with the Holy Spirit. The baptism in the Holy Spirit brings the church into the same place of spiritual authority, and provides it with the same spiritual resources, as the infilling of the same Spirit gave Christ.

It should be as easy for us to cast out demons as it was for him, with the exception that not every Christian is individually called to engage in this ministry. No single Christian can be all that Jesus was. He was the complete Apostle-Prophet-Evangelist-Pastor-Teacher (Ep 4:11).

Individually, we can reflect only a small part of this full ministry. But collectively, the church is made into the "body" of Christ, with Jesus as Head, and this "body" should convey to the world the same ministry Christ himself would fulfil if he were here. Each local church should in effect be Christ in its neighbourhood, offering in his name healing and deliverance to those who live around it.

2.   The Extent Of Demonisation In Society

I have already drawn attention to the remarkable number of demoniacs described in the gospels, in contrast to the remainder of the NT, and to the OT. No fully satisfactory explanation has yet been offered for this situation. But there may be some truth in the suggestion that there was a sudden surge of overt demonic activity during the years of Jesus' incarnation. The idea is that the kingdom of darkness concentrated its forces on Palestine in hope of destroying Christ before he fulfilled his mission.

Whatever the reason, there does not seem to be the same measure of demonic penetration in our society. The number of recognisable demoniacs seems to be much less than those encountered by Jesus. Perhaps the influence of the church is a factor here. The presence of righteousness, the abolition of many fears, the preaching of Christ, the prayers of the saints, may all serve to inhibit satanic oppression in our society. The devil may be driven to attack people today in ways other than demonising them - perhaps in more subtle ways, through pride, materialism, sensuality, unbelief, and the like.

Missionaries have often reported that the level of overt demonic activity on the foreign field is much higher than in their home countries. There are many demon-possessed people in so-called Christian lands, but the incidence of demonisation appears to be much lower than that recorded in the gospels.

3. An Indirect Authority

Although Christ depended on the anointing of the Holy Spirit when he healed the sick and cast out demons, nonetheless he had a direct authority that is not given to us, or at least, not in the same way. Because he was filled with the Spirit, he could act in his own name, and, by virtue of his unique identity as "Son of God", overthrow the powers of darkness. Even the demons recognised this, and often revealed who he was - "*What have you to do with us, Jesus of Nazareth? Have you come to destroy us? I know who you are, the Holy One of God*" (Mk 1:24; 5:7; etc.).

However, we cannot speak in our own name, nor any other, except that of Jesus himself. Even then, our use of his name must be based on a vital personal relationship with him. Sceva's sons were savagely beaten, and fled bruised and naked, when they tried to exorcise a demon using the formula, "*I adjure you by the Jesus whom Paul preaches!*" (Ac 19:13-17). The demonised man was not delivered; but there was still great gain for the church -

> "*fear fell upon all (who heard about this), and the name of the Lord Jesus was extolled ... So the word*

of the Lord grew and prevailed mightily" (vs. 17,20).

4. The Laying-On Of Hands

Just as there is no record that Jesus ever laid hands on a demonised person, so there is no specific statement that the disciples ever did so. There are in fact only four instances where scripture reports the method of exorcism used by the disciples -

> *"We saw a man casting out demons in your name" (Lu 9:49) ... "Lord even the demons are subject to us in your name!" (10:17) ... "I charge you in the name of Jesus Christ to come out of her" (Ac 16:18) ... "Handkerchiefs and aprons were carried away from Paul's body to the sick, and diseases left them and the evil spirits came out of them" (19:12).*

You will notice that in three of those examples the only method used was a spoken command in Jesus' name. There is no indication that laying-on of hands was employed. The fourth example is hardly one that can be copied. Luke acknowledges that even for Paul it was "extraordinary" for people to be delivered merely by contact with a cloth the apostle had touched (vs. 11).

I cannot prove that the disciples never laid hands on the demonised, only that there is no specific record of them doing so. However, it might be inferred that demonised people were among those whom the disciples did heal by laying hands on them - see Ac 5:12; 14:3; 19:11; etc.

With or without the laying on of hands, the name of Jesus, spoken in the power of the Holy Spirit, was the main agent by which the early church expelled demons. And that use of his name was linked with a simple spoken command, such as, "I tell you to come out, in the name of Jesus!" Nothing more was needed. Anything more exposed unbelief. So did failure to achieve the desired result.

The disciples tasted both. They had great success (Mk 6:13); they experienced humiliating failure (9:18). When they succeeded,

Jesus warned them not to be too elated, not to be carried away by the drama and exhilaration of driving out demons, not to start believing in themselves, but to keep their faith firmly where it belonged - fixed in heaven, and on the grace of God that had saved them (Lu 10:20). When they failed, Jesus bluntly told them to blame their own unbelief - see Mt 17:19-21; Mk 9:27- 29.

5. Ministering To The Demonised

How should you minister to someone who is demonised?

When the time comes, take authority over the demon in the name of Jesus, and firmly command it to leave. Never waver in your confidence that it must and will obey your command (Mk 16:17).[77]

Sometimes you may need to move in immediately, and begin at once to pray for the afflicted person. But usually it is better to insist that people first ground themselves in scripture, and in a sense of their own spiritual authority in Christ. Have a list of positive scriptures ready for them to study and pray over, until irresistible faith rises in them.

But remember that the name of Jesus cannot be used like a pagan talisman; you cannot turn it into an empty incantation. Faith is what counts; not merely mouthing certain pious words.

Fasting may also be useful, especially as an aid to faith (Mt 17:21; Mk 9:29).[78]

---

[77] If you doubt the genuineness of this verse, as part of the so-called "longer" ending of Mark, note that it is referred to by Justin (c. 160), Tatian (c. 170), and by Irenaeus (c. 200). Even if it were not an original part of Mark's gospel, it accurately reflects an early church consensus about the Great Commission.

[78] Don't think about fasting as a key to power over demons. It is not. Whatever authority we have over demons comes solely from our union with Christ by faith, not from some pious work. The two verses I have

6. Overcoming Oppression/Depression

There is no reason to assume that a state of oppression or depression has a demonic cause, nor that being in such a state is a sign of spiritual failure. Even Jesus experienced such times (He 5:7-8; and cp. his anguish in the Garden of Gethsemane).

Before resorting to exorcism to solve the problem (which won't work, anyway, if there is no demon to expel!), try the following:

♦ refuse to worry about either the depression or its source; unless the cause is obvious to you, trying to track it down is probably futile.

♦ refuse to allow the depression to control you; but resolve, as nearly as you can, to live a normal life, continuing to fulfil your ordinary duties.

♦ refuse to feel guilty about being depressed; recognise it as something artificial, an outside invader, lying on the surface of your life, not representing your true self.

♦ accept that this depression, with its cynicism, doubt, and the like, cannot touch your inner spirit, where true faith still resides, and the Holy Spirit still imparts his regenerating life.

♦ know that this depression cannot grip you indefinitely; you will break through it in Jesus' name (even if it does have a demonic origin); so do not yield to anxiety or despair.

♦ don't make the mistake of trying to fight against it, which only gives it a kind of legitimacy. When you focus your attention on depression you tend to establish it, to give it recognition, a de facto right to inhabit you. The more you

---

quoted in this place are also doubtful. Mt 17:21 is probably not an original part of the gospel, but was added by a later hand, perhaps in the second century. Likewise, the words "and fasting" are missing from many ancient copies of Mark (9:29).

struggle against it, the stronger it is likely to become. You give it muscle by wrestling with it. It is usually better simply to "ride it out", as a ship does a storm. But you can certainly take a stand against the devil, and insofar as he may have a hand in your problem, exercise full authority over him in the name of Christ.

♦ the best antidote to depression, indeed to any affliction, is a rich knowledge of your God-given identity in Christ, with all the good opinion of yourself that flows out of the gracious things God affirms of you in Christ.

You will have victory over Satan when you are rid of self-doubt, when you do not depend on secondary authority (as the sons of Sceva tried to do), and when you have rooted your confidence in the reality of your union with Christ, in his resurrection, ascension, and enthronement.

I don't often go to demons for a lesson, but it is hard to escape the impact of their assertion, "We know!" If those sons of Sceva had the right words to say, and the right faith to confess, and the right authority to exercise, they would not have been humiliated. So know who you are in Christ, and act accordingly!

III. PROFESSIONAL EXORCISM

With varying degrees of enthusiasm and commitment, exorcism has been practised in the church from the time of the apostles until today. Around 200 AD the office of exorcist was formally established for the first time - perhaps in an attempt to stop the shocking abuses that had developed. Irresponsible charlatans had brought disgrace upon the church and threatened to destroy the true ministry of exorcism. From that time the practice of exorcism was increasingly restricted to those who were licensed to do so. This is still the rule in some of the older denominations.

But heresy seems never to be far removed from those who devote their ministry to exorcism. There is something innately unhealthy about focusing all one's attention upon demons.

I have already mentioned that the word "exorcism" is not once used of Jesus or of the apostles, despite its great familiarity to the people of that time. The early church did not want the label "exorcists" hung upon their pastors and evangelists. This is because four things characterised the common exorcist, things that the church sternly disavowed –

A. PROFESSIONALISM

The exorcists specialised in, and were paid for, casting out demons. That was their ministry; that is how they made their living. They developed a wide range of esoteric techniques and mystical formulae. The early church rightly poured scorn on such mumbo-jumbo -

> "A diseased affection is not destroyed by a counter-affection, nor is a maniac cured by hanging little amulets of leather upon him ... (They are) the elemental matter with which the depravity of the demons works, who have determined for what purpose each of them is available. And when they see that men consent to be served by means of such things, they take them, and make them their slaves.. "[79]

> "Now assuredly your exorcists, as I have said, make use of craft when they exorcise ... and employ fumigations and incantations ... (But) every demon,

---

[79]   Tatian, op. cit., ch. 17. Tatian's comments on demons are spread over three or four chapters. He refers to many of the superstitious practices of the exorcists and healers; their use of roots, herbs, incenses, and even organs taken from cadavers, both human and animal.

when exorcised in the name of (the) very Son of God ... is overcome and subdued ... (For) he said, `I give unto you power to tread on serpents, and on scorpions, and on centipedes, and on all the might of the enemy.' And now we, who believe on our Lord Jesus ... when we exorcise all demons and evil spirits, have them subjected to us."[80]

I cannot say it is quite wrong to specialise in a ministry of exorcism; but there is no warrant for such a narrow focus in scripture. Observation shows that those who do concentrate on a single aspect of scripture (whether demonology, eschatology, or any other) seem to be driven into ever greater excesses of either doctrine, or practice, or both. At least let this be said: beware of professional exorcists, whether Christian or otherwise.

B. SUPERSTITION

1. Some Examples

The exorcists developed a "lore" of demons, an amazing compilation of superstitions, rules, formulae, rituals, and the like. For example: the number of demons is 7.5 million; they are able to assume human form, except they have feet like a hen, or like a goat, and they cast no shadow; they reveal their presence in secret ways, known only to an expert; special magic alone can exorcise them; they yield only to an exact sorcery - a single mistake in the spell, the slightest omission from the routine, would invalidate all; a demon can be expelled by learning its personal name, and then repeating the name, omitting one syllable at a time, with each omission weakening the demon's strength; and so on.

That last practice deserves special comment –

---

[80] Justin Martyr, Dialogue With Trypho, ch. 85 & 76; op. cit. Notice that Justin adds "centipedes" to the original passage from Luke.

2. The Name Superstition

The idea is still widespread that knowledge of a demon's name will enhance an exorcist's control over it. There is no basis in the NT for such a belief. Yet many modern exorcists repeat the errors of their forerunners, spending much time and effort developing ways of compelling a demon to name itself.

The origin of this belief is not Christian, but pagan. The Babylonians, for example, sought to identify and name every demon. One of the common ideas in the ancient world was that knowing the name of a spirit or god gave special powers to the possessor of this knowledge. Secret words or formulae were also thought to be a source of control over demons. I have observed some modern exorcists who seem to place the name of Jesus, or certain phrases from the Bible, in the same category. But that holy name and those sacred words are not voodoo mutterings. Do you suppose the mere saying of words - any words - will oblige a demon to flee? Authority comes not from words but from faith.

I have also noticed that the names given to demons by the ancient pagans were based on the same kinds of evidence used by some Christian exorcists: revelations, dreams, utterances by the demon through its victim, various physical manifestations, and the like. Those heathen roots surely make the practice suspect.

a. The example of Jesus

Someone may object that Jesus himself sought the name of a demon before he expelled it. The only place where evidence of this can be found is in the account of the demoniac of Gadara (Mk 5:9; Lu 8:30). Note that Jesus addressed his question to the man himself, not to the demon, and the reply may have surprised him: "My name is Legion!" Anyhow, several things are obvious:

♦ Christ had no need to know this demon's name, in order to expel it. Named or unnamed, every demon was obliged to obey his plain command.

- The name given (Legion) was scarcely a sensible identification; it says nothing about the nature of the demons involved, indicating only that they were "many".

- There is no other instance of Jesus showing any interest in the name of a demon (with the possible exception of Beelzebul; but that had no connection with exorcism.)

- He made no use of the name Legion, nor of any other name, when expelling the evil spirits possessing the Gadarene. He treated them as one company, and bade them all leave the man together. According to Matthew, Jesus said only one word; a thrilling "Go!" Trembling with terror, the demons hastily obeyed (8:32).

There is no other example in the NT of a demon being given a proper name. Demons are placed rather in certain categories:

- unclean (Mk 3:11); evil (Lu 7:21); deaf (Mk 9:25); divination (Ac 16:15); infirmity (Lu 13:11); lying (1 Kg 22:22); fear (2 Ti 1:7).

But such categories scarcely represent proper names. All demons may be classed as "unclean" and "evil". Also, the adjectives are linked more with the afflictions suffered by the victims, than with the demons themselves. The Bible is also ambiguous in its terminology, using different adjectives to describe identical demons. Mark calls the demon afflicting the epileptic boy "a dumb and deaf spirit" (9:25); Matthew says simply a "demon" (17:18); and Luke, "an unclean spirit" (9:42).

b. The early church

Arnobius (c. 300) reveals the low opinion the Fathers had of all these superstitious practices -

> "My opponent will perhaps meet me with many other slanderous and childish charges which are commonly urged. (Such as), Jesus was a Magian; he effected all these things by secret arts; from the

shrines of the Egyptians he stole the names of angels of might, and the religious system of a remote country. Why, O witlings, do you speak of things which you have not examined, and which are unknown to you, prating with the garrulity of a rash tongue? Were, then, those things which were done (by Jesus) the freaks of demons, and the tricks of magical arts? Can you specify and point out to me any one of all the magicians who have ever existed in past ages, that did anything similar, in the thousandth degree, to Christ? Who has done this without any power of incantations, without juice of herbs and of grasses, without any anxious watching of sacrifices, of libations, or of seasons? ... And yet it is agreed on that Christ performed all those miracles which he wrought without any aid from external things, without the observance of any ceremonial, without any definite mode of procedure, but solely by the inherent might of his authority."[81]

How pure and uncluttered the ministry of Jesus! That is the example you should strive to follow, having nothing to do with silly superstitions and pagan rituals.

c. Fear

A third tool of the professional exorcist was (and is) fear. Exorcists love to stress the idea of demon possession, with its connotation of helplessness, and its corollary that only a skilled exorcist can bring deliverance. Who else has the special revelation? Who else knows the right formula? Who else has sufficient knowledge and power to expel the

[81] Against The Heathen, Bk. 1; ch. 43 & 44. "Ante-Nicene Fathers," Vol. 6

demon? Indeed, the trade of the exorcist, whether Christian or pagan, depends upon promoting fear of demons. Never tell people their freedom is in their own hands! Never tell them they have no need of the exorcist!

d. Mysticism

Professional exorcism thrives on promoting a sense of drama. There must be excitement and high emotion. Victory should not come too quickly, and certainly not easily. Rather let there be bitter struggle, prolonged conflict. Let the act of casting out a demon be seen to require heroic spiritual effort! Thus the exorcist enhances his reputation. Thus he makes the victims of demons ever more dependent upon him.[82]

---

[82] Here are a couple of charming accounts of professional exorcism in 10th century Japan. They are taken from The Pillow Book Of Sei Shonagon, tr. Ivan Morris; Penguin Classics, 1967. Sei Shonagon was a lady-in-waiting at the emperor's court. Her book is a lively record of things in daily life that pleased and displeased her.

"The lot of an exorcist is still more painful. On his pilgrimage to Mitake, Kumano, and all the other sacred mountains, he often undergoes the greatest hardships. When people come to hear that his prayers are effective, they summon him here and there to perform services of exorcism; the more popular he becomes, the less peace he enjoys. Sometimes he will be called upon to see a patient who is seriously ill and he has to exert all his powers to cast out the spirit that is causing the affliction. But if he dozes off, exhausted by his efforts, people say reproachfully, `Really, this priest does nothing but sleep!" Such comments are most embarrassing for the exorcist, and I can imagine how he must feel." (Pg. 26)

"With a look of complete self-confidence on his face an exorcist prepares to expel an evil spirit from his patient. Handing his mace, rosary, and other paraphernalia to the medium who is assisting him, he begins to recite his spells in the special shrill tone that he forces from his throat on such

How different was the ministry of the apostles! Their practice gave no hint of the foolishness endemic in much professional exorcism, both ancient and modern. They knew the real authority of Jesus' name. They scorned the use of ritual words and repeated formulae. They depended on faith alone.

Exorcism needs to be de-mystified. It should be one of the easiest aspects of Christian ministry. Seizing and maintaining personal victory over satanic power should be one of the surest possessions of every believer.

IV. EXORCISM IN THE EARLY CHURCH

Justin Martyr

> "For (Jesus) was made man also, as we before said, having been conceived according to the will of God the Father, for the sake of believing men, and for the destruction of the demons. And now you can

---

occasions. For all the exorcist's efforts, the spirit gives no sign of leaving, and the Guardian Demon fails to take possession of the medium. The relations and friends of the patient, who are gathered in the room praying, find this rather unfortunate. After he has recited his incantations for the length of an entire watch, the exorcist is worn out. `The Guardian Demon is completely inactive,' he tells his medium. `You may leave.' Then, as he takes back his rosary, he adds, `Well, well, it hasn't worked!' He passes his hand over his forehead, then yawns deeply (he of all people!) and leans back against a pillar for a nap." (Pg. 41,42. A "watch" lasted two hours.)

Ivan Morris adds the following footnote -

"The aim of the exorcist was to transfer the evil spirit from the afflicted person to the medium, who was usually a young girl or woman, and to force it to declare itself. He made use of various spells and incantations so that the medium might be possessed by the Guardian Spirit of Buddhism. When he was successful, the medium would tremble, scream, have convulsions, faint, or behave as if in a hypnotic trance. The spirit would then declare itself through her mouth. The final step was to drive the spirit out of the medium." (Pg. 280)

learn this from what is under your own observation. For numberless demoniacs throughout the whole world, and in your own city, many of our Christian men exorcising them in the name of Jesus Christ, who was crucified under Pontius Pilate, have healed and do heal, rendering helpless and driving the possessing devils out of the men, though they could not be cured by all the other exorcists, and those who used incantations and drugs."[83]

"For we call him Helper and Redeemer, the power of whose name even the demons do fear; and at this day when they are exorcised in the name of Jesus Christ ... they are overcome. And thus it is manifest to all, that his Father has given him so great power, by virtue of which demons are subdued to his name."[84]

Irenaeus

"For they (the heretics and pagans) can neither confer sight on the blind, nor hearing on the deaf, nor chase away all sorts of demons - except perhaps those that are sent into others by themselves, if they can do even as much as this. Nor can they cure the weak, or the lame, or the paralytic, or those who are distressed in any other part of the body, as has often been done in regard to bodily infirmity. Nor can they furnish effective remedies for those external accidents which may occur. And so far are they from being able to raise the dead, as the Lord raised them, and the apostles did by means of prayer, and

---

[83] Apology, ch. 6; op. cit.

[84] Dialogue With Trypho, ch. 30; ibid.

as has been frequently done in the brotherhood on account of some necessity - the entire church in that particular locality entreating with much fasting and prayer, the spirit of the dead man has returned, and he has been bestowed in answer to the prayers of the saints - they do not even believe this can possibly be done, but hold that the resurrection of the dead is simply an acquaintance with the truth which they proclaim ..."

"Those who are in truth (Christ's) disciples, receiving grace from him, do in his name perform miracles ... For some (according to the gift which each one has received from Christ) do certainly and truly drive out devils ... Others have foreknowledge of things to come: they see visions, and utter prophetic expressions. Others still, heal the sick by laying their hands upon them, and they are made whole. Yea, moreover, as I have said, the dead even have been raised up, and remained among us for many years."[85]

Tertullian

" ... the very advocates (in your courts) ... are themselves also under obligation to us ... The clerk of one of them who was liable to be thrown upon the ground by an evil spirit was set free from his affliction; as was also the relative of another, and the little boy of a third. How many men of rank (to

---

[85]   Against Heresies, Bk. II.xxxi.2 & xxxii.4; op. cit.

say nothing of common people) have been delivered from devils, and healed of diseases."[86]

---

[86] To Scapula, ch. 4; op. cit. Tertullian gives similar testimony to the power of the early church over sickness and demons in Apology, 23 & 27; and To Scapula, ch. 2.

CONCLUSION

Now I must end these chapters. Rather abruptly, I regret, for I am far short of saying all that should have been said.

I believe in angels. I believe in Satan. I believe in demons. Angels I revere, as my fellows in the service of God. Satan I respect; but not with any fear, for Christ has already given us mastery over him, and I know that "the God of peace will soon crush Satan under our feet" (Ro 16:20).

Demons we may scorn. Their defeat is total. Satan we may have to "resist"; demons we are told simply to "cast out" (1 Pe 5:8-9; Mk 16:17-18).

The things discussed in these chapters are great mysteries. Experience shows that experience is a very unreliable guide in unravelling these mysteries. It is best to stay as close as possible to scripture. Speculation may soon become superstition. Practice based on experiment may soon become irresponsible fanaticism.

We must take seriously the mission God has given his angels "to serve those who are to obtain salvation" (He 1:14) - but it is unwise to go looking for an angel. We must also take seriously the mandate Christ has given the church to cast out demons - but let caution, good sense, and scripture prevail.

Now Paul can have the last word -

> *In all these things we are more than conquerors through him who loved us. For I am sure that neither death, nor life, nor angels, nor principalities, nor things present, nor things to come, nor powers, nor height, nor depth, nor anything else in all creation, will be able to separate us from the love of God in Christ Jesus our Lord (Ro 8:37- 39).*

BIBLIOGRAPHY

Ancient Near East, The; Vol. II; ed. J. B. Pritchard; Princeton University Press; 1975.

Ante Nicene Fathers; *William B.Eerdman's Publishing Co., Grand Rapids, Michigan; 1979.*

Believer's Bible Commentary; William Macdonald; Thomas Nelson Publishers; 1989.

Bible Background Commentary; Intervarsity Press, Nottingham, UK; 1993.

Bible Knowledge Commentary, The; by John Walvoord and Roy Zuck; Cook Communications, Colorado Springs, Colorado; 1989.

Calvin's Commentaries; John Calvin (1509-1564).

City of God, The; Augustine (1467); tr. Henry Bettenson; Penguin Classics; 1977

College Press NIV Commentary, The; Joplin, Missouri; 1996.

Commentary on Ephesians, A; Charles Hodge (1797-1878).

Commentary on the Bible; Adam Clarke (1715-1832).

Commentary On The Old And New Testaments, A; John Trapp (1601-1669).

Commentary on the Old and New Testaments, A; Robert Jamieson, A. R. Fausset, David Brown; 1871.

Commentary on the Old Testament, Vol. 1, The Pentateuch; William B. Eerdman's Publishing Co., Grand Rapids, Michigan; 1976 reprint.

Dictionary of the Christian Church, The; *ed. J. D. Douglas,* Art. Zoroastrianism; *Paternoster Press; Exeter, Devon, U.K; 1974.*

Encyclopaedia Britannica; 1963 edition.

Explanatory Notes on the Whole Bible; John Wesley (1703-1791).

Exposition of the Entire Bible; John Gill (1690-1771).

Expositor's Bible Commentary, The; ed. Frank E. Gaebelein; Zondervan Publishers, Grand Rapids, Michigan.

Expository Commentary; H.A. Ironside (1876-1951).

Greatness That Was Babylon, The; H. W. F. Saggs; Sidgwick & Jackson, London; 1969;

Holman New Testament Commentary; ed. Max Anders; B & H Publishing Group, Nashville, Tennessee; 2004.

Interpreter's Bible, The; Abingdon Press, New York; 1952.

IVP New Testament Commentary Series, The; Intervarsity Press, Nottingham, UK.

Jewish New Testament Commentary; David H. Stern; Jewish New Testament Publications, Inc., Clarksville, Maryland; 1982.

Marriage Of Heaven And Hell, *The Voice of the Devil*; William Blake (1790-1793)

Matthew Henry's Commentary; Marshall, Morgan, and Scott, London; 1953.

Matthew Poole's Commentary; 1685.

Nelson's New Illustrated Bible Commentary; Thomas Nelson Inc., New York; 1999.

New Testament Commentary; *The Gospel of John*; William Hendriksen; Baker's Publishing House, Grand Rapids, Michigan; 1987.

Notes on the Bible; Albert Barnes (1798-1870).

Notes on the New Testament; by Kregel Publications; Grand Rapids, Michigan. reprint, 1966

People's New Testament Commentary, The; B. W. Johnson; Word Search Corporation, Nashville, Tennessee; 2010.

Pillow Book Of Sei Shonagon, The; *tr. Ivan Morris; Penguin Classics; 1967.*

Plutarch's Lives, *tr. by John Dryden, Modern Library edition, published by Random House, New York; undated*

Poor Man's Commentary On The Whole Bible, The; Robert Hawker; 1850.

Portable Milton, The; Penguin Books, New York; 1982.

Preacher's Commentary, The; Word Inc., Nashville, Tennessee; 1992.

Preacher's Outline and Sermon Bible; Word Search Corporation, Nashville, Tennessee; 2010.

Pulpit Commentary, The; ed. Joseph S. Exell, Henry Donald Maurice Spence-Jones; 1881.

Theology of the Older Testament,The; Dr. J. Barton Payne; Zondervan Publishing House, Grand Rapids, Michigan; 1975 reprint.

Vincent's Word Studies; Marvin R. Vincent; 1886

Week On The Concord And Merrimack Rivers, A; The Heritage Press, Norwalk, CT; 1975.

What Luther Says, *Vol One; compiled by E. M. Glass; Concordia Publishing House, St Louis, MO; 1959.*

Wiersbe's Expository Outlines; Warren W. Wiersbe; Publisher, David C. Cook, Colorado Springs, Colorado.

Word Pictures In The New Testament; A. T. Robertson; 1933.

Wycliffe Biographical Dictionary of the Church; Elgin Moyer (1890); revised Earle E. Cairns; Moody Press; Chicago; 1982

www.ingramcontent.com/pod-product-compliance
Lightning Source LLC
Chambersburg PA
CBHW060741100426
42813CB00027B/3018